About the Authors

City Lit, based in London, is the largest adult education college in Europe, providing thousands of part-time courses each year, from the visual and performing arts, to languages, humanities, complementary therapies, and counselling.

City Lit's Faculty of Deaf Education and Learning Support offers one of the most comprehensive programmes in Europe for D/deaf learners and those interested in working in a deaf-related field. With over 60 years' experience, the provision is nationally and internationally viewed as a centre of excellence, and the department is frequently contacted to offer advice, support and training on a wide variety of issues related to deafness, deaf learners, and working with deaf people.

Learners come from all over the country and beyond – so unique is the programme and so highly regarded are the expertise and skills of staff (who are D/deaf, hard of hearing, and hearing). The team includes teachers of the deaf, of lipreading and sign language; teacher trainers, interpreters, communicators, note takers (manual and electronic) and hearing therapists.

City Lit's annual Deaf Day celebration is a free national event providing a large exhibition and many exciting workshops. Usually held in March or April, it is open to all. For more information please visit www.citylit.ac.uk

Melinda Napier is Deaf from birth and comes from a Deaf family. She has worked at City Lit for over 25 years, managing the Communication and Training Programme Area. She has taught on Teacher Training courses since 1981and has vast experience of teaching BSL from Level 1 to Level 4. She was with the Association of British Sign Language Tutors and Assessors from the very start and is now its Chair. She lives in Surrey and loves London, her children and new Australian granddaughter. She is living in the hope that her granddaughter will learn from the book to communicate with her grandmother in BSL not AUSLAN (Australian Sign Language)!

James Fitzgerald has been working within the faculty of Deaf Education at City Lit for the past 9 years. In that time, he has worked as a note-taker, a communication support worker, a lip-speaker, a support tutor and now as a qualified BSL/English interpreter. In addition to interpreting, James co-ordinates the faculty's Business Training & Interpreting Unit and delivers deaf awareness and communication courses with a Deaf colleague to staff at City Lit, and to external businesses around London. Apart from BSL, James has a love of log-fires and wellington boots, and lives in leafy Surrey with his wife and four kids . . . and seven ducks!

Elise Pacquette (the illustrator) attended Norwich School of Art and Design, where she studied for a BA (Hons) in Illustration, and an MA in Fine Art. Whilst working as a prop maker in London, she started learning BSL. She has worked at City Lit since 2002 as a Senior Communicator and is currently studying a PGDip in BSL/English interpreting. She lives in London with her husband and two young children and regularly receives painting commissions to fit into her free (!) time. She loves baking, singing, painting, and (oh, yes) signing.

Authors' Acknowledgements

With a huge thanks to all the staff and students from the City Lit Faculty of Deaf Education and Learning Support whose contributions and support have been invaluable in putting together this resource. We are confident that all new learners of BSL will not only benefit from their hard work but will also enjoy themselves learning the language of the Deaf community in Britain!

Publisher's Acknowledgments

We're proud of this book; please send us your comments through our Dummies online registration form located at www.dummies.com/register/.

Some of the people who helped bring this book to market include the following:

Acquisitions, Editorial, and Media Development

Project Editor: Simon Bell

Technical Reviewer: Charles Herd

Content Editor: Jo Theedom

Copy Editor: Kim Vernon

Publisher: Jason Dunne

Executive Editor: Samantha Spickernell

Acquisitions Editor: Nicole Hermitage

Executive Project Editor: Daniel Mersey

Cover Photos: © Vikki Martin/Alamy

Cartoons: Ed McLachlan

Composition Services

Project Coordinator: Lynsey Stanford

Layout and Graphics: Stacie Brooks, Nikki Gately, Melanee Habig, Erin Zeltner

Proofreader: Laura Albert

Indexer: Johnna VanHoose Dinse

Publishing and Editorial for Consumer Dummies

Diane Graves Steele, Vice President and Publisher, Consumer Dummies

Joyce Pepple, Acquisitions Director, Consumer Dummies

Kristin A. Cocks, Product Development Director, Consumer Dummies

Michael Spring, Vice President and Publisher, Travel

Kelly Regan, Editorial Director, Travel

Publishing for Technology Dummies

Andy Cummings, Vice President and Publisher, Dummies Technology/General User

Composition Services

Gerry Fahey, Vice President of Production Services

Debbie Stailey, Director of Composition Services

Contents at a Glance

Table of Contents

Introduction

You may have seen people signing in the streets, restaurants, or shops and didn't know what they were saying. Perhaps you wondered whether they were using proper language or just miming. You may have heard of *Deaf culture* but didn't know what the term meant. You may have bought this book because you want to learn signing and communicate with a deaf person you know, a work colleague, or a neighbour so here is your opportunity to learn their language and be able to hold basic conversations with them.

Whatever the reason why you're reading this now, *British Sign Language For Dummies* introduces you to basic sign language and helps you get an understanding of Deaf culture. You cannot learn sign language without understanding a bit of Deaf culture as they go hand in hand, and once you understand both, you become a better signer.

About This Book

This book focuses on British Sign Language (BSL) with some simple explanations of grammatical rules. We assume you bought this book because you want to learn BSL, not to learn about grammatical jargon in depth. There are plenty of books around that explain the linguistics aspects of sign language.

Like any spoken language, BSL has regional signs and dialects. For this book, we have chosen the most common signs, the ones that are understood all over the UK.

This book is categorised according to subject. You can use each chapter as a building block for the next chapter, or you can skip around wherever you please. Just choose a subject that interests you and dig in. Just remember that it is fun to learn BSL and you can practise with your friends. Don't worry if you couldn't get the hang of it, just keep on practising and your Deaf friends will help you.

Conventions Used in This Book

To help you navigate through this book, let us explain some conventions we've used when writing this book:

 ✔ Whenever we use a sign in lists, examples and dialogues, we print the word version of the sign in capital letters to show that it's the closest equivalent to its English counterpart.

 ✔ When we are about to introduce a new sign, we print it in **bold** in the text, so that you know you're about to learn a new sign.

 ✔ We capitalise the letter **D** in the word Deaf whenever it means culturally Deaf (explained in depth in Chapter 1)

 ✔ The text for both signs and English always come before the equivalent illustrations.

 ✔ The illustrations have arrows on them to show the direction of the sign. A wavy line indicates that the fingers of the signing hand wiggle up and down. See the sign for 'when' on page 36.

 ✔ To save space, words that are fingerspelled do not have illustrations, and you can refer to Chapter 1 or Cheat Sheet if you need help remembering how to sign a letter or number.

 ✔ Web sites appear in `monofont`.

This book also includes a few elements that other *For Dummies* books do not have. The elements that you'll find are as follows

 ✔ **Starting To Sign:** Seeing signs in actual context in the text and on the CD helps you understand how to sign the dialogues in correct grammatical order.

 ✔ **Fun & Games activities:** These visual games help you practise your signing skills and are a good way to have fun while checking your progress; and you can have more fun if you practise this with a friend.

The English sentences are translated into British Sign Language (BSL) and are not to be taken as word-for-word translations.

Foolish Assumptions

We hate to assume anything about anyone, but when writing this book, we had to make a few foolish assumptions about you. Here they are (we hope we were right):

 ✔ You have little or no experience in this type of communication, but you have a genuine interest.

 ✔ You don't expect to be a fluent signer after learning from this book. You just want some basic signs in simple sentences.

 ✔ You want to learn about the grammatical rules of BSL, but in a practical way, rather than by spending hours learning theory.

┃ ✔ You want to learn a few signs in order to be able to communicate with
┃   Deaf friends, family members and colleagues.

How This Book Is Organised

This book is divided by topics into parts, then divided into chapters. The following sections let you know what kind of information you can find in each part.

Part I: Starting to Sign

This part introduces you to the concept of communicating with different
groups of Deaf people with a range of hearing losses, and how to attract
their attention, as well as looking at some principles of good communication.
Chapter 2 helps you to understand fingerspelling and how to make sense of
signing and facial expressions.

Part II: Everyday BSL

In this part, you learn how to communicate with Deaf people using basic
signs and sentence structure. You will be able to ask and understand simple
questions, express and recognise basic facial expressions.

Part III: Getting Out and About

All the signs you need from giving directions, making plans, meeting friends
and getting around are in this part.

Part IV: Looking into Deaf Life

Read this part to learn about Deaf history of education, community and
culture as well as finding out how Deaf people use technology to get better
access to information.

Part V: The Part of Tens

Here you can find useful tips to help you improve your signing skills. This
part gives you ideas for good communication and helps you overcome any
uncertainty you may feel. You'll also be amazed by some information you
didn't know about Deaf people.

Part VI: Appendixes

This book has two appendixes. Appendix A gives you all the answers to the Fun & Games questions. Appendix B gives you detailed instructions for playing and using the CD that accompanies this book.

Icons Used in This Book

To help you find certain types of information more easily, we've included several icons in this book. You find them on the left-hand side of the page, sprinkled throughout:

This icon gives the handy hints and tricks of the trade that can make signing easier.

This icon emphasises important information that you should take away with you.

This icon warns you to avoid making a mistake or offending a Deaf person, so take note of what these paragraphs have to say.

This icon highlights useful tips about BSL grammar rules.

This icon helps you to understand bits of information about the culture of the Deaf people.

This icon highlights the text that you also find on the CD. Many Starting To Sign dialogues appear on the CD, so you can practise with other signers.

Where to Go from Here

The beauty of this book is that you can go anywhere you want. You may find it helpful to start with the first two chapters to get down the basics, but if that's not your thing, feel free to jump in wherever you want. Find a subject that interests you, start signing, and have fun!

Part I
Starting to Sign

The 5th Wave   By Rich Tennant

"I never thought I'd have to say this, but this is a public library. Please tell your friends to keep their signing to a whisper."

In this part . . .

This Part gets you up and running with BSL. We talk in detail about the different sorts of people with hearing loss, and introduce you to the basic ground rules for good signing communication.

We also show you a few basic signs, including the BSL signs you already knew without realising.

Chapter 1

Discovering Who's Who – And How They Communicate

*1*n this chapter, we talk about the different terms used to describe people who don't hear. This is the starting point of good communication – getting the descriptions right. We look at the differences between those who describe themselves as 'deaf' (with a small 'd') and those who use 'Deaf' (with a big 'D'). We look at the variety of communication tactics which you can use with different groups, and show that not all deaf people sign, and not all deaf people lipread. Knowing what's what and being flexible will make a big difference to your whole experience of communication.

Different Groups of Deaf People

Terminology is changing all the time – that's what happens with all living languages. In any subject there may be words that become commonly used, and those that go out-of-date . . . and some that no longer carry their original meaning at all and can even become offensive.

Who's dumb?

Deaf-related terminology changes like that of any other language. Take 'deaf and dumb', for example, which was originally used to mean someone without hearing or speech. Decades ago, this was a common term and there were 'schools for the deaf and dumb'. Older people may still use this term, but its meaning has now changed and the term can cause offence. Dumb now has another meaning, 'stupid', and nobody wants to be called stupid! There may be many reasons why a deaf person chooses not to use their voice – one of them being that they are a BSL user's – and BSL is not a spoken language. Deaf-mute is also not used. It may be more appropriate to say 'deaf without speech' if the deaf person has chosen to use other methods of communication. True 'muteness' is a different matter and is not directly related to deafness.

Generally unacceptable terms to describe deaf people include: deaf and dumb, deaf-mute, stone deaf, Mutt and Jeff, special needs (a better term might be 'have special requirements' or 'additional requirements/support'), non-hearing (what woman would call herself non-male, for example?) and anything with '-challenged' at the end.

Understanding who's who

So what about other terms? What terms used to describe deaf people are generally acceptable to use now, and what do they mean? The following sections cover some terms and their descriptions that you may find useful.

deaf

When you use the word *deaf* (with a small 'd') you're referring to anyone with a hearing loss, for whatever reason, and at whatever level. The term is mostly used by deaf people who use methods *other than* sign language to communicate.

Out of a population of about 60 million, there are approximately 9 million in the UK who have a hearing loss to some degree. That's 1 in 7 of the population!

Deaf

Deaf (with a capital 'D') is quite a different matter, and refers to the Deaf community. Just as we might use capital 'B' for British or 'A' for Australian, so a capital 'D' is used to show that this is about a person's identity, not about their medical condition. The defining characteristic of a Deaf person is that they use BSL as their first or preferred language. People who are Deaf often share a common 'Deaf culture' which includes Deaf history, education, clubs, social events, sports (such as the Deaf Olympics) as well as sign language. Those who do not use sign language would not use the capital 'D' (unless of course it's at the start of a sentence!). Sometimes you may see the term **D/deaf** which includes those who are 'hearing impaired' as well as those are part of a linguistic minority group (BSL users).

BSL is the first or preferred language of about 70,000 Deaf people in the UK.

You can be part of the Deaf community without actually being Deaf yourself. A CODA is a Child Of Deaf Adults who is hearing, but raised in the Deaf community by parents who are Deaf. A CODA is likely to be bilingual – switching easily from BSL to spoken English, but may consider BSL to be their first language.

Hard of hearing

Hard of hearing is not just a term for an old person who may be losing their hearing. You can be hard of hearing at any age for many reasons. The term tends to refer to someone with a mild or moderate hearing loss. Hard of hearing people might rely on the hearing they've got (residual hearing), and use technical devices such as hearing aids and loop systems to amplify the sound. A HOH person may also be relying a lot on lipreading to communicate, and has possibly joined a lipreading class to help them with this. More often than not, someone who is HOH has lost their hearing later in life, in any regards after they have acquired language. So a hard of hearing person is, a lot of the time, said to have an 'acquired hearing loss' rather than a 'congenital' one (i.e. born deaf).

Out of 9 million people in the UK with a hearing loss of some degree, approximately 8.3 million of these are 'hard of hearing'.

Hearing impaired

Hearing impaired is a generally acceptable term used to describe someone who has a hearing loss. It could refer to someone who is born deaf, or became deaf later in life. Some people prefer the term 'hearing impaired' to being described as 'deaf', especially if they are relying on residual hearing.

The term 'hearing impaired' would *not* be used by someone who is Deaf (with a capital 'D'), as he or she is part of a Deaf cultural community, and doesn't consider himself or herself to be 'impaired' by their deafness.

Deafened

We might say 'that music was deafening' if it's particularly loud and those with so-called 'selective hearing' might say they are 'deafened' to the sound of your voice. But this term also refers to a unique group of deaf people – those who have suddenly lost their hearing (normally in adulthood) and have acquired a severe or profound level of deafness. This might be caused by several things, including noise damage (for example a bomb blast, or industrial noise), a trauma to the head (such as a car accident), an illness, or even a severe reaction to medication. Of course, the cause might also be unknown. A deafened person has perhaps not had any time to get used to losing their hearing. It could even happen overnight. Imagine if that happened to you, how your life would change. Your ability to communicate with your family, friends, at work, on public transport . . . everything will have been affected. You can no longer hear the radio, the TV, use the phone, or hear that double-glazing salesman at the door (some would say that's the only advantage!). If you suddenly lose your hearing, you won't automatically know how to lip-read – it's not something you've ever had to do. You're also unlikely to want to learn BSL – what would be the point, if your family or friends don't know how to sign?

One of the other challenges with being 'deafened' is that other people may have no idea you have a hearing loss. After all, your voice would stay the same; there'd be no issue with your speech. You may not wear hearing aids, as they can take a while to get used to, and some deafened people might be concerned about the stigma of wearing them. It's not as if you'd be wearing a bright pink t-shirt saying 'I'm deafened', so others are likely to be completely unaware and babble on regardless. This can cause a huge amount of frustration and bewilderment, which is why 'deafened' people are in a group of their own. They have unique communication requirements, and support needs.

There are approximately 150,000 deafened people in the UK

Deafblind

Deafblind is the term used to describe someone with a dual sensory loss – it could be that a person was deaf and lost their sight later, or blind, and lost their hearing later. Or they may have been hearing and sighted and lose effective use of both senses later in life. Due to immunisation against *Rubella*, it's becoming rarer for a child to be born both deaf and blind (the main cause was the mother contracting *Rubella* while pregnant). Someone who is part of the Deaf community (see above) and loses their sight (maybe due to a syndrome called 'Usher') would write Deafblind (with a capital D), for the same reasons as given above.

In the UK, there are approximately 24,000 registered deafblind people.

. . . And how do they communicate?

The preferred method of communication for a deaf person will usually depend on which of the main groups he or she belongs to. The following sections walk you through each of these preferred methods.

Deaf (capital 'D')

British Sign Language! The language of the Deaf community in the UK . Presumably you're reading this book because you want to learn to sign. Well this is the group to practise with. Don't go practising your signs on anyone who happens to be wearing a hearing aid. It's only **D**eaf people who use BSL as their first and preferred language, in Britain. Unless they've learned the language for another reason, anybody else won't know what you're on about, and might think you're performing a mime act.

If you want to communicate with a Deaf BSL-user, and you don't use BSL yourself, try to think visually. Use some more gestures (as appropriate) and communicate more with your face. Raise your eyebrows to ask questions, nod to show you have understood, shake your head to indicate 'no' . . . and smile if you're saying something positive! Deaf people are pretty good at reading your body language and facial expressions, so limber up and show what you mean to say! Keep using the English language but avoid using long complex sentences or jargon, and keep to the point.

For Deaf Sign Language users, English may not be their first language. It can be pretty difficult to lipread a language you don't know well.

Don't switch your voice off and stop moving your lips when talking to a BSL user (unless you're using BSL yourself). Even if English is not their mother tongue, the Deaf person will want to get information from your lips and may benefit from hearing some sound from your speech to accompany lipreading – if they have some residual hearing or use hearing aids.

You don't need to gesture everything! Just key points, to get your message across. If you're asking about their Christmas holidays, you don't need to perform a whole Nativity play to get across the word 'Christmas'. Don't labour it – just find another way of saying 'Christmas' – for example, 'December the 25th' (showing 2 and 5 on your hands). You can always write down key words too!

Hard of hearing

If they use English – keep using English. But don't use BSL for this group. Keep using your voice, and be aware that a hard of hearing person will most likely be lipreading you. Some hard of hearing people will have attended lipreading classes, and may be making effective use of recognising speech patterns. However, even the best lipreaders only get a maximum of about 30 per cent from lip-patterns alone. Lipreaders take in information from body language, facial expressions, the context and other clues to make informed decisions about what a phrase or word might be on the lips. It can take a lot of skill and a lot of experience, and can be extremely frustrating for the lip-reader, but there are things you can do to make lipreading much more effective. See the section below for some lipreading tips.

A hard of hearing person may also use various pieces of equipment to help with communication. Depending on their type and level of deafness, they may find a loop system helpful, or may use radio aids or other amplification systems. Sometimes it may help if you speak up a little bit – but don't shout! Shouting will distort your lips and could give you an aggressive facial expression. And who likes to be shouted at anyway? Speaking more clearly is much more effective. Something to bear in mind: there's really no need to exaggerate your lips. Rubber lips not only make you look peculiar, they don't help with lipreading either! Keep it natural.

Deafened

If you suddenly lose your hearing, you will naturally try to lipread, but lipreading is likely to be hard work and exhausting, especially if you are recently deafened. For some deafened people, lipreading is just too difficult, so the main communication choice would be the use of pen and paper. But remember – there's not a problem with language . . . so you don't need to simplify your English. Just write everything down, as normal. Just because you've lost your hearing, doesn't mean you've lost your language too. A deafened person will normally respond using their own voice. So if you shout to make yourself understood, you might get shouted at in reply!

Don't go heavy on the gestures and animated facial expressions with a deafened person. Just use natural gestures. A deafened person is quite unlike a visually-communicative Deaf signer, and if they're stereotypically English, they're not going to be comfortable expressing themselves with wild gesticulations, and will not thank you for doing so either. It's also hard to lipread if you're used to a stiff upper-lip!

Deafblind

How a deafblind person communicates depends on lots of things – their level of deafness and blindness, as well as on when they became deaf or blind. Someone born blind who then loses their hearing would use different forms of communication to someone born deaf who then loses their sight. A Deaf BSL-user who loses their sight later in life is still a member of the Deaf community, and might want to keep using BSL so may use 'hands-on BSL' by putting their hands over the person signing to feel the movements. The person they are talking to would need to modify their signing slightly to compensate for the fact that their facial expressions (an important part of BSL) cannot be seen clearly.

A lot of deafblind people choose to communicate using the 'deafblind manual alphabet' which is BSL fingerspelling modified so that it is done onto one hand of the deafblind person, who reads it through touch. Some 'signs' are also made into the palm as shortened ways of saying things such as 'yes' and 'no' or 'again'. Some deafblind people can pick up deafblind manual at more than 80 words per minute, without the need to pause between words. Of course, not everyone can spell that fast, but many deafblind manual interpreters may operate at that speed. If the person has a good knowledge of English, full sentences are spelled out onto the palm. If English is not their preferred language, the same rules apply as if you're writing on paper – everyday words, to the point, simple sentences and not too much waffle. Yes – you can still waffle using deafblind manual!

So what if you were to meet a deafblind person, and wanted to communicate with them? Let's say you don't know hands-on BSL, you can't get your fingers around deafblind manual, and there's no-one else nearby who's learnt it either. What would you do? No running off! If you know how to write and you've got fingers, you have all you need. You can use the standard alphabet, and spell out words into the palm of the deafblind person's hand. It's called the 'block manual alphabet'. Write in capital letters – it's much easier to distinguish through touch. And make sure you spell out each word properly – one letter on top of the other. Don't go writing essays over their whole body, up the arms and down the legs. They might not thank you for that, and worse . . . they might be ticklish.

Spell out words properly – don't abbreviate to 'U R' instead of 'you are' – as this way has only really been developed from texting. Don't worry if you make a mistake – you can always rub it out! (but not with a rubber . . . and certainly not with tippex!)

Attracting a Deaf Person's Attention?

There's no point in saying 'excuse me' 'now listen . . .' or 'Oi you!'. They won't hear you. And don't be tempted to say 'are you deaf, or what?'. In this situation, you know the answer.

There are several ways of getting a D/deaf person's attention – some ways are more suited to a particular situation, and it depends also on how well you know the person. The important thing is: get the D/deaf person's attention BEFORE you start speaking. It's no good getting their attention *while* you're talking – it will take a few moments for the D/deaf person to register your face, adjust themselves to you, the light, and the environment. So allow a few moments before you start speaking, otherwise your first few words or sentences might be lost, and the conversation will have started off on a bad footing. Here are a few ways you might try:

Touching on the arm or shoulder

If you know the person, and you know they are comfortable with this, then touching them lightly on the arm or shoulder might be a perfectly okay way of getting their attention. If you don't know them, you might want to be cautious about using touch – some people are not comfortable with it, for personal, social or cultural reasons. Also – be careful not to grab or startle someone with a sudden touch. You might end up with a black eye.

Don't grab a Deaf person's arm to catch their attention if they are signing. It's the equivalent of sticking your finger in someone's mouth while they're talking!

Waving

Not the Mexican type. More a gentle wave of the arm to catch their eye. Half-way between an air-traffic control signal and a gentle butterfly motion should do the trick. If they don't see you, move a little closer. Don't just stand there waving. You might attract the unwanted attention of some bird-spotters.

Stamping on the floor

Never one-to-one, unless you're two years-old and having a tantrum. But in a Deaf school, the teacher might use this method to get the attention of the whole class. It saves time having to wave at each student – by the time you've got the last person's attention, you've lost it with the first lot. So sometimes stamping the feet is used, as vibrations are sent through the floor, and every-one turns to face the teacher at the same time. Not to be recommended on concrete floors, however. You might just break your foot.

While stamping on the floor or banging on the table might be something famil-iar within Deaf culture in schools, it's not used in the mainstream – unless you want to come across as angry or impatient. So within a group of hard of hearing people, in a lipreading class perhaps, the teacher would not use this means to get the class's attention. It could easily offend!

Switching the light on and off

This works well to get the attention of a group of people who have a hearing loss. It's always best to establish this way with the group at the outset, or people could think there's a problem with the electrics, or that you're trying to set up a disco. Flashing lights are very much a part of Deaf culture, as they are a visual way of getting attention – whether as a fire alarm, door bell, or to signify the start of a presentation or class (as in a Deaf school).

Watch My Lips!

Lipreading is used as a communication tool for a large number of deaf people, including Deaf BSL users who are communicating with those who don't sign. In fact, everyone uses lipreading to an extent. Have you ever tried to hold a con-versation with someone through a closed window? Or across a crowded pub (did he say 'do you want a *pint of coke*', or 'do you want to *buy a goat*'?). You may have noticed that when you can't quite hear what someone is saying, your eyes will automatically flick down to their lips, and you will try to lipread. Try it yourself by watching the news on TV with the volume turned down a bit. You will notice that it's easier to lipread if you can hear some sound – even if only a little. So a good tip to help lipreading . . . keep using your voice (unless you're using BSL) as it will enable the lipreader to match lip-patterns with the sounds of the word, if they have some residual hearing.

Lipreading on its own is hard work. As mentioned above in the section on 'hard of hearing', lipreading is greatly assisted by other clues apart from just the lips. One of the reasons lipreading can be so difficult is that much of what we say is not clearly identifiable on the lips. Sounds such as 'C' as in *car* and 'G' as in *garden* are not visible on the lips at all. Other sounds can look very similar eg. M/P/B (mark/park/bark); as well as F/V (fingers/vicars) or Cr/Gr (crab/grab), T/D/S (tie/die/sigh), and W/Qu (white/quite). A simple gesture, an appropriate facial expression or knowing the context can make all the difference in the world, or you could end up with 'sausages and *passion*' instead of 'sausages and *mash*' and a 'pint of *milk*' instead of a 'pint of *beer*'.

Don't presume someone can lipread just because they don't hear. Although some become very skilled at it, others may find lipreading impossible and never get the hang of it. There could be many reasons for this – maybe English is not their first language or they are recently deafened. Like anyone, they may be tired, ill, distracted, or fed-up. They might not understand your lip-patterns, can't get used to your accent (which affects the way you move your lips!), or you might have a big bushy beard or mumble your words. They could just be having a bad day. Or it could be that they don't like looking at your face!

Making yourself more lipreadable

When speaking to a lipreader you can make life simpler for them – and yourself – by following a few simple rules.

- ✔ **Keep your hands away from your face:** Don't obscure your lips with a book, newspaper, or lollipop, either.

- ✔ **Get rid of the chewing gum:** It's nearly impossible to lipread while someone's chewing, drinking, or puffing on a cigarette.

- ✔ **Face the lipreader when you're talking to them:** You don't need to stare them out, but do try to maintain eye-contact throughout your conversation.

- ✔ **Don't over-exaggerate your lips:** It'll make lipreading much more difficult and makes you look odd.

- ✔ **Don't shout!** It won't help, it will make you look angry, and will distort your lip-patterns

too. Better to raise your voice slightly, if with someone who is hard of hearing, and try to speak more clearly.

- ✔ **Move your lips more:** If you're someone who speaks like a ventriloquist, you do need to make your lip movements clearer. This will make your speech clearer and ensure that there is more lipreading going on, and less mind-reading.

- ✔ **Get the light right:** Be careful not to stand in front of the window, as this will put your face in shadow. Even the best lipreaders can't lipread in the dark; and the flashing lights of a nightclub might be a bit of a distraction too. Having said that, most hearing people can't hear conversations in a nightclub as the music's too loud, so lipreaders are possibly at an advantage in this environment!

Chapter 2

Sign Language You Didn't Know You Knew

In This Chapter

▶ Using gestures and natural signs

▶ How to finger-spell and read finger-spelling

▶ Handy hints on hand shapes

▶ BSL grammar as it is signed

*Y*ou may think that signing is going to be difficult to pick up as you've never used your hands to describe something before. Think again! Signing is not all that difficult once you've picked up the basic rules. Using your hands and facial expressions instead of your voice may seem strange at first but with practice you will get used to it. This chapter shows you how to use your fingers, hands and face to get your meaning – and feelings – across.

Signs That Make Sense

If you think you don't use your hands when talking and that only excitable foreigners wave their hands about when communicating, you're mistaken.

Gestures

When talking with someone you use gestures naturally to show things such as boredom (palm of hand tapping open mouth) delight (thumbs up) or strange behaviour (forefinger tapping temple).

If you find yourself in a noisy environment, or a window is between you and a person you're trying to communicate with, you may mime 'phone me', 'drink?' or 'smoke?' and be easily understood. When angry, you may wag your finger at a person or use a jabbing movement.

See! You do use your hands to communicate!

So, what is a gesture? A gesture is a movement, usually unconsciously made, to convey meanings, describe sizes, or add emphasis to verbal statements.

Think of as many gestures as possible that you use. Here's a few to start off with: 'hi!' (hand raised in greetings), 'goodbye' (hand waving), 'baby' and 'swim'.

How do you sign this word?

You use your hands to convey or emphasise meanings, sometimes deliberately and sometimes unconsciously. Gestures and signs have been in existence as long as people have communicated. Cavemen probably used them when indicating to their friends the size of the fish they had just caught or the woolly mammoth they had fought single-handedly.

Iconic or natural signs, such as those for **baby, eat, drink** and **drive** are as clear to a non-signer as verbal communication.

BABY: Mime rocking a baby in your arms.

EAT: Mime putting food into your mouth.

DRINK: Mime drinking from a tumbler.

DRIVE: Mime using a steering wheel to drive a car. (Note: can also be used for 'CAR')

Not all gestures and signs are clear, for example, the sign for **book** is not immediately obvious but, once someone has explained and demonstrated, you see the obvious link between the hands, the shape of the book and how the book is used.

BOOK: Hands represent opening and shutting a book.

TELEPHONE: You've seen this sign in many TV adverts, your thumb and little finger represent the handset of a telephone.

Don't assume that all signs correspond to gestures or can be easily recognised. Some signs are quite obscure as they do not look like the word they represent. **Can** and **aunt** provide good examples of this.

CAN

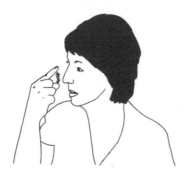

How does BSL create new signs?

As with spoken languages, BSL constantly creates new signs – as when a new phrase comes into the language or new equipment such as mobile phones,

DVD recorders, webcams and satellite TV come into being. The symbols usually come from how you use the items or what they look like.

Some signs have undergone change over the years, **telephone** is an excellent example.

TELEPHONE: This sign was used in the 1920s and 1930s.

 The sign for telephone may be used differently among different age groups. A few of the older generation would probably use the one shown here whereas younger people may sign it the same way as a mobile phone is used.

The majority of sports signs are iconic. See Chapter 11 for sports signs.

Making It Clear with Body Language

Hopefully, you have realised by now that communicating in British Sign Language (BSL) is a matter of using your fingers, hands and arms. What you may not have fully realised yet is the importance of facial expressions and body language to accompany the signs. For example, the sign **don't know** is much clearer when accompanied by a shrug. Another example is **no**, which is simply a shake of the head but can be given varying degrees of emphasis by the accompanying facial expression.

Let Me Spell It Out: Finger-spelling

One sure way to communicate with deaf people who sign (remember not all deaf people sign) is by finding out how to fingerspell. Communication solely through finger-spelling is slow at first, in the same way that it would be slow if you had to spell out every word you spoke, but it can be a useful, and possibly vital, skill to acquire.

Finger-spelling is the positioning of the fingers on the hands to form the 26 letters of the English alphabet and is used to convey personal names, names of places and other words that people don't use frequently enough to have acquired a sign of their own.

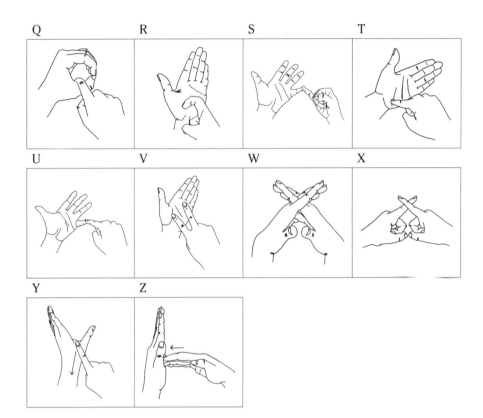

When using finger-spelling, remember the following:

- ✔ Don't switch hands
- ✔ Keep your hands fairly close together
- ✔ Keep your elbows by your sides
- ✔ Watch the signer's lips, not their fingers

Left or right?

Not switching hands means that if you're right-handed, the right hand does all the spelling on the left hand and vice versa. Switching hands interrupts the pattern of the spelling and confuses the person who is being spelled to.

People who have not been brought up using this skill, or who are acquiring it but do not have regular contact with Deaf people who would provide them with the opportunity to practise, find it more difficult to master because, as with most things, practice makes perfect.

Actually, you can probably acquire the finger-spelled alphabet in an hour or so. However, the 'reading' of it – that is, understanding someone who is finger-spelling to you – is the difficult part.

Watch my lips – not my fingers

You may well ask how you can see the letters being spelled on the hands if you're not watching them but, in the huge majority of cases signers also mouth the word they spell at the same time so, because you can also see the fingers in your peripheral vision, you have two visual inputs to help you. You almost certainly need to watch the signer's fingers to start with, but as you become more skilled you can focus more on the lips.

Now you see it, now you don't

In order to understand more easily, remember that you do not need to 'see' every letter in a word to understand it. Take the following words for example:

_ L _ PHANT

IND _ P_ND _ NT

All the 'E's are missing but you can guess 'Elephant' and 'Independent' because of the positions of the other letters.

What could this word be?

B O _ T S

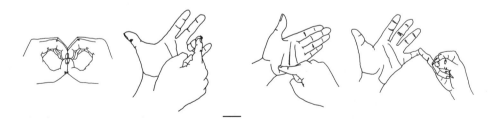

If this word was spelled to you and you failed to pick up the third letter you would be faced with several choices: 'boots', 'boats', 'bolts' or 'bouts'. However, if you put the word into the context of a signed sentence such as, 'I must buy a pair of Wellington boots', 'I love watching sailing boats', 'The door has very strong bolts' and 'He has frequent bouts of coughing' you can guess the word easily.

Can you read this?

Aoccdrnig to a rscheearch at Cmabrigde Uinervtisy, it deosn't mttaer in what odrer the ltteers in a wrod are, the olny iprmoatnt thnig is that the frist and lsat ltteer be in the rghit pclae. The rset can be a taotl mses and you can stlil raed it wouthit porbelm. Tihs is bcuseae the hmuan mnid deos not raed ervey lteter by isetlf, but the wrod as a wlohe. Amzanig huh?

The same principle applies to fingerspelling. If you pick up a few of the letters in a word, including the first and last ones, you can usually make an educated guess at what the word is.

You must remember that, on average, only about one word out of maybe one hundred in a signed sentence is actually finger-spelled, so the context of the sentence usually helps identify the word.

In this book a word or name that is finger-spelled is shown in hyphenated letters. For example: John is written as J-O-H-N. You can find the 'signs' for the alphabet in this chapter as well as the Cheat Sheet at the front of this book.

When you were small and finding out how to write, you probably wrote 'd o g', 'c a t', 'b a l l', and so on, as separate letters. As you got older, you got used to writing using 'joined up letters'. The same principle applies to finger-spelling, you need to spell words in a continuous movement rather than as one letter after another. The word 'wing' for example is spelled by starting with the 'W', moving your index finger over to the 'I', sliding it down the finger to the 'N', then carrying on the movement to the 'G'. Spelling the month of 'May' you would start with the 'M', move your index finger up the front of the thumb to the top for the 'A', then move it down the back of the thumb to the 'Y'.

Funny Faces

BSL is not just manual signing with hands. You obtain equally important information from face and body, which can be used to modify or emphasise the meaning of a sign.

For example: you can use or emphasise **you** in different ways such as **Who are you?**; **It was you!**; **You?**; (in disbelief) **You? No, it can't be!** (The last one is accompanied by a shake of the head.)

Using funny faces

Stand in front of mirror, preferably when no one is looking if you want to avoid funny looks. Try looking surprised by raising your eyebrows, or raise just one eyebrow – think Roger Moore, basically. Never mind whether you feel foolish. Hopefully no one is watching, and you will soon get the hang of it.

No! Not me!

A facial expression can be used to show negation in different ways. You probably use a shrug of the shoulders when saying **don't know**, or you may use a frown with a shake of the head for **Not me!** or **No, that's wrong!**. These negative facial expressions can be used on their own or with accompanying signs.

You can also change the meaning of a sign from positive to negative by using a headshake. In the phrase **I'm not happy**, you sign **happy** but shake your head with a frown while signing.

Oh yes!

Yes is just a nod of the head and is usually a reply to a question or to confirm a statement such as **I'm deaf**, **I work here** or **I enjoyed my holiday**.

Are you happy?

Pay attention to your facial expressions, they show people how you feel about the information you're giving them. For example, if you sign the word **miserable**, show a sad expression and your shoulders slumped. When you sign **happy**, show the opposite with a smile and raised shoulders.

Be careful how you use facial expressions as they can be misunderstood. If you wear a smile when signing **miserable**, people may think they've misunderstood you – or send for the men in white coats!

You can find more information about facial expressions in Chapter 5.

Getting Your Hands into Shape

In this book, all the illustrations represent a right-handed signer.

You can use various hand shapes to make up signs. If you're right-handed, use your right hand as the dominant one, making most of the signs in the air or on the passive left hand, and vice-versa for a left-hander.

What is a hand shape?

A sign is usually made up of a hand shape, or two combined, a movement and a location and they can be used to show how we handle and use objects, as well as representing people and their movements.

Use a flat hand shape to represent flat surfaces such as a floor, wall, door, box, shelves, and so on, and to show a moving vehicle – car, lorry, bus, or motorcycle.

FLOOR

WALL

DOOR

MOVING CAR

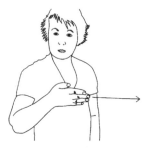

A person is represented by an upright forefinger and by turning it and moving it about you can show the person facing you, facing away from you, approaching you, walking away, walking sideways, and so on.

FACING YOU

MOVING AWAY

Use a 'V for victory' hand shape – but facing downwards – to show the legs of a person and what she is doing – **walk**, **stand**, **sit**, **fall**, **kneel**, **jump**, **hop**, and so on.

STAND   **JUMP**   **WALK**

You can use the same hand shape – held in front of the face – to represent 'eyes' for signs such as **watch**, **look**, **look up**, **look down**, **stare**, (accompanied by a look of concentration), and so on.

LOOK   **LOOK UP AND DOWN**

You can modify a sign to show different meanings by using facial expressions of varying intensity. The hand shape of a sign remains the same but you change the movement and facial expressions to show the differences in, for example, for **cold**: chilly, cold, and freezing. Another example is **wind**, the facial expression can show a gentle breeze, strong wind, gale, and so on.

Simple Sentences: Sign Order

In English grammar the word order in a sentence is more often subject-verb-object. In sign language the order is usually topic-comment. The main or important item of information often starts the sentence, for example, 'New car I bought yesterday'; 'Holiday in Scotland next week' rather than ' I bought a new car yesterday' and 'I am going to Scotland next week for my holiday'.

Chronological order

Sometimes the sentence starts by giving the time when an event has happened or will happen, for example, ' Last month bought new car', 'Next week holiday in Scotland'.

Question forms

The structure of the sentence often changes, especially with 'Wh' questions (which involve the words 'who', 'what', 'when', 'where', and 'why')' or Yes/No questions, and is made at the end of sentence.

See Chapter 3 for the nitty-gritty of question forms.

Fun & Games

What are these phrases? The answers are in Appendix A.

1.

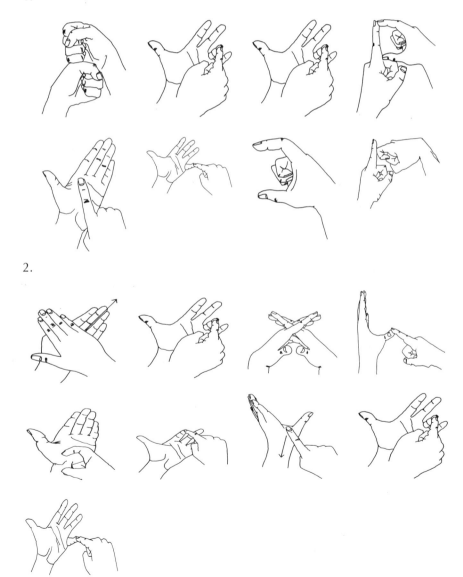

2.

3.

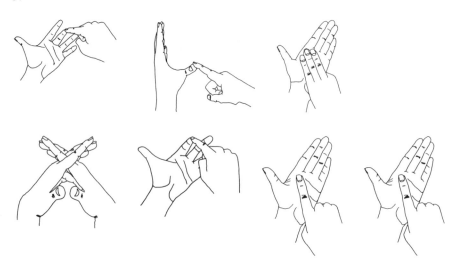

Two-lettered words

Try to build your skills by doing this activity – think of and spell as many two- lettered words as you can – here are a few to start you off:

am   go   to   by

Palindromes

Now try this. Spell the following words then see whether you can spell them backwards – an example is given below. Remember to keep the letters 'joined up'.

WAR	RAW	PAT	_ _ _
SAW	_ _ _	BUT	_ _ _
TON	_ _ _	NIB	_ _ _
WON	_ _ _	PIN	_ _ _
NOD	_ _ _	DOG	_ _ _
POT	_ _ _	BAT	_ _ _
RAT	_ _ _	NAP	_ _ _

Part II
Everyday BSL

The 5th Wave   By Rich Tennant

"I think what she's saying is even a deaf person can't sign over _that_ shirt."

In this part . . .

Here's where you need to be to get to grips with talking to Deaf people using basic signs and sentences. This Part helps you ask and understand simple questions, and express and recognise basic facial expressions.

The chapters in this part take you through the nitty-gritty of day-to-day BSL communication, including signs to help you with everything from meeting and greeting through talking about health issues, to chatting about the weather and what to wear.

Chapter 3

Meeting and Greeting

*I*n this chapter, you get an idea of how to greet, start a conversation with and take leave of a Deaf BSL user. Even if you only know a few signs, you can hold a brief conversation. When you've started to pick up a few signs, you will want to meet Deaf people and practise your newly acquired skills. Attending a BSL class is the best way to pick up BSL, but if that is not possible, you may be able to attend a Conversational Club at a Deaf Club where you can meet Deaf BSL users and others finding out about BSL to practise your signing skills.

No signer has the same style of signing. Speakers of a spoken language have different ways of using words. The same is true for sign language, the signs remain the same but how people sign them can differ.

Greetings! Starting a Conversation

Generally when you meet someone, you start by saying 'Hi', 'Hello', 'How's life', or something like that, then you start conversing. The examples in this chapter give you a helping hand – or fingers.

Do you worry about how to approach a Deaf person and start a conversation? When people meet for the first time, they usually start by introducing themselves, then follow up with questions to find out about the other person. With the signs in this chapter, you can do the same with a BSL user. How to approach? You can start by signing **hi** or **hello** if he is facing you; if not, tap on a shoulder or wave your hand in his eye line to get his attention, then sign **hi** or **hello**.

You need to know the difference between informal and formal ways of greeting. For an informal greeting, you add the sign **good** after signing **hi**/**hello**.

HI/HELLO (formal)

HI/HELLO (informal)

If you see Deaf people signing in the street and want to talk to them, do not necessarily expect them to be pleased to see another signer and welcome you into their conversation. They may be having a private conversation and not want another person present.

If you see someone signing outside, the best way to approach them is to say sorry for the interruption and ask for directions using BSL (even if you know perfectly well where you are and where you want to go). If their reaction is lukewarm, do not press further but, more often than not, they ask whether you're Deaf. Be honest and say you can hear but know a few signs. Usually they are happy to answer your questions and may even ask you questions themselves.

Asking questions: Who? What? Why? When? Where? Which? How?

In spoken languages, people depend on the tone of voice to give specific meanings to their speech. For example, you can make the statement 'You're working tomorrow' into a question 'You're working tomorrow?' or a command 'You're working tomorrow!' by the tone and emphasis of your voice.

In BSL, 'You're working tomorrow' can be made into a question or a command by using different facial expressions and the use of a question sign.

The type of question is indicated by both the use of the eyebrows and a question word – What, Who, Where, When, Why, Which, or How being placed at the end of the sentence.

WH questions (open)

We call questions using interrogative signs and requiring information from the other person (like **where, who, what, which, when, why,** and **how)** *WH questions.* When signing WH questions, use lowered/knitted eyebrows, a slight narrowing of the eyes and the head tilted forward or sideways slightly to show that you're asking a question and need information. In such cases, you will expect the answers to be longer than a short 'yes/no' (closed question), for example, 'What do you do?' – 'I'm a bus driver'.

In BSL, you almost always sign WH question signs at the end of sentences, for example: 'Your name what?', 'You live where?', but they can occasionally occur at the beginning, for example: 'What happened?', 'Where from?'.

Not all people can raise their eyebrows – even if they haven't had had Botox injections– in this case, a slight tilting of the head forward or sideways should be sufficient to convey the meaning.

Knitted eyebrows with head tilted forward

Look at the WH questions in Table 3-1.

Table 3-1		WH Questions	
English	*Sign*	*English*	*Sign*
WHAT		WHEN	
WHY		WHERE	
WHO		WHICH	

Yes/no questions (closed)

Yes/no questions require the other person to respond with only a short answer, often just a 'yes' or 'no', for example: 'Are you married?' – 'Yes', 'Want a cup of tea?' – 'No'.

In BSL, signers indicate questions that require a yes/no answer by raised eyebrows and head tilted back.

RAISED EYEBROWS WITH HEAD TILTED BACK

Rhetorical questions

A rhetorical question does not require an answer and is asked only for effect. Signers indicate a rhetorical question by raised eyebrows and head tilted back, for example: 'And do you know what he did? he went ahead anyway'.

Getting to Know You

Say you've plucked up the courage to approach a Deaf person and greeted them. If not familiar with you, he may ask you whether you're Deaf, do not be taken aback if he asks you this question – the enquiry is a compliment. He may think your signing is good enough for you to be a Deaf person.

Never pretend to be Deaf, just to be able to practise your signing. A Deaf BSL user will soon see through you and – like Queen Victoria – not be amused and possibly make an excuse and disappear. Be honest and he will probably give you practice, but don't monopolise someone too long. You may have practised your school French on people when holidaying abroad and remember their pained expressions.

DEAF	HEARING	SIGN

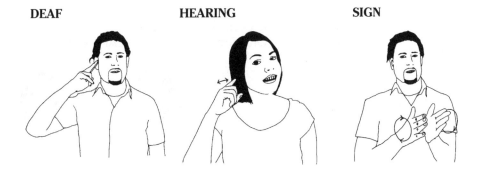

In BSL, when signing **you** and **me**, never actually say the words. Don't make any mouth movement and you just point to yourself or the other person.

You may have been brought up to think that pointing is impolite but in BSL pointing is necessary as it shows the listener to whom or what you are referring.

Starting to Sign

Olga sees Mark signing with Peter and approaches them.

| Olga: | Hello! |
| Sign: | HELLO |

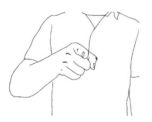

| Mark: | Are you Deaf? |
| Sign: | YOU DEAF? |

| Olga: | No, I'm hearing and you? |
| Sign: | (Shaking head) NO ME HEARING. YOU? |

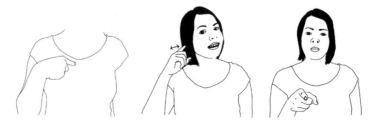

Mark: I'm Deaf. Can you sign?
Sign: ME DEAF. YOU SIGN?

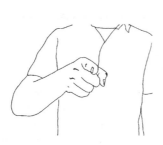 

Olga: I know a little bit.
Sign: LITTLE.

Name sign? What's that?

Deaf people often give each other name signs and often create them from the appearance, a characteristic, or the behaviour of that person. A name sign helps Deaf people to identify who you're talking about without you having to resort to fingerspelling their full name. Personal name signs may change over time. Deaf people may have allocated name signs to each other when they were at school together but they may have changed as they grow older or they meet other Deaf people who give them new ones, for example, a boy at school may have been given a name sign that depicted his long curly hair, but may then have gone bald at an early age. People with names, especially surnames, that are common English words such as Brown, King, and so on, usually have name signs for the sign of that particular word. For examples: Peter Brown can be signed as **P. Brown** and Alan King as **A. King**.

What's in a Name?

During introductions, simply *fingerspell* (sign each letter individually) your name. Deaf people often give each other *name signs*. Those who can hear, the hearing, don't invent their own, nor do they give name signs to each other. (See the nearby sidebar for more on what exactly name signs are.)

NAME

In BSL, when signing 'What's your name?' (**name what?**), never say the word 'what'. When signing **what**, don't make any mouth movement, just point to the person whose name you're giving or asking for.

Where do you live?

Not all towns and cities have their own name signs, so many signers use fingerspelled abbreviations. Because of local and regional variations in signs, many different signs often exist for the same place so, if you see a sign you do not recognise, do not be afraid to ask.

Some towns and cities have their names fingerspelled using just a few their letters – spelled quickly in a familiar pattern – which represents the whole name. For example: you can sign Manchester as M-C, Newcastle N-C, Oxford O-X, and Glasgow G-W.

Cities/towns such as Blackpool, Chester, Swansea, and so on, use the common signs for **black**, **chest**, and **swan** to identify them. Others use signs associated with the city, such as **noise** (London, a noisy place), **knife** (Sheffield and cutlery), **pistol** (rhymes with Bristol), and **bow and arrow** (Robin Hood – Nottingham).

LIVE

Starting to Sign

 John and Olga start to introduce themselves.

Mark:	I'm Mark . What's your name?
Sign:	(pointing to self) M-A-R-K. (pointing) NAME?

Olga:	I'm Olga.
Sign:	(pointing to self) O-L-G-A

Mark:	I live in Manchester. Where do you live?
Sign:	ME LIVE M-C. (pointing) LIVE WHERE?

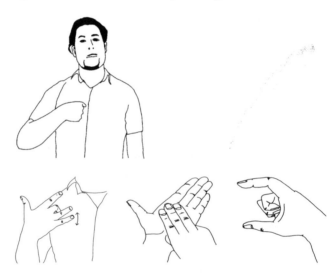

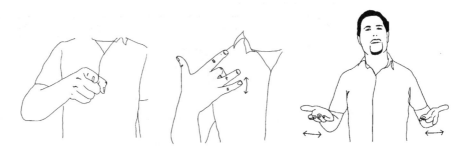

Olga:	I live in Newcastle.
Sign:	(pointing to self) LIVE N-C

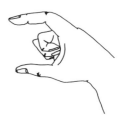

You can see some of the common signs for towns and cities in Table 3-2.

Table 3-2	Signs for Towns and Cities		
English	**Sign**	**English**	**Sign**
LONDON		BRIGHTON	
BIRMINGHAM		LIVERPOOL	

(continued)

Table 3-2 *(continued)*

English	Sign	English	Sign
SWANSEA		EDINBURGH	
CARDIFF		LEEDS	
WOLVERHAMPTON		PORTSMOUTH	
NOTTINGHAM		CAMBRIDGE	
SHEFFIELD		HARTLEPOOL	

Starting to Sign

 Olga is telling Mark about the cities she has lived in before.

Olga: I have lived in many different cities.
Sign: ME BEFORE LIVE MANY CITY

Mark: Really, where?
Sign: REALLY, WHERE?

Olga: I have lived in Liverpool, Leeds, Sheffield, and Nottingham

Sign: ME LIVE LIVERPOOL, LEEDS, SHEFFIELD, NOTTINGHAM

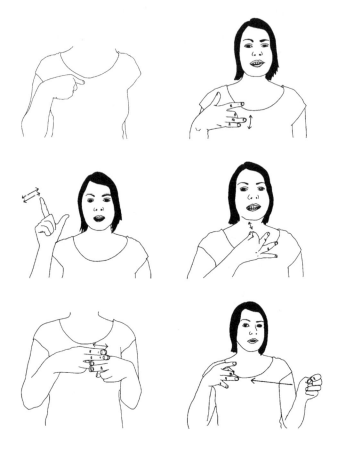

Mark: You live in Newcastle now?
Sign: YOU LIVE N-C NOW?

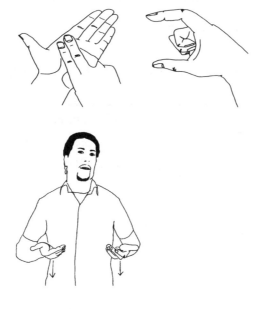

| **Olga:** | Yes, that's right. |
| **Sign:** | (Head nod) RIGHT. |

So Long, Farewell, Auf Wiedersehen, Goodbye

Deaf BSL users have different ways of taking leave, depending on the situation and depth of friendship. Don't be surprised to find yourself being hugged and given a kiss on the cheek; regard this gesture as a compliment as it means that you've been accepted as 'one of them'. Handshaking is more formal but Deaf men, when meeting their male friends or taking leave, usually shake hands then give a quick hug and pat their backs.

Ways of ending a conversation depend on who you're talking to. Look at the following signs to help you to end a conversation appropriately.

The sign for **goodbye** is simply a wave, which is no different from the one hearing people use.

See Table 3-3 for various examples of signs for taking leave of someone.

Table 3-3		Taking Leave		
English	**Sign**		**English**	**Sign**
GOODBYE/ BYE			BETTER	
GO			SOON	
SEE			AROUND	

Starting to Sign

Olga and Mark take leave of each other.

Olga: I'd better go now. See you around.
Sign: (pointing to self) BETTER GO NOW. SEE AROUND.

 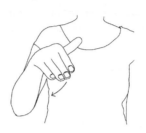 

Mark: Goodbye. See you soon.
Sign: GOODBYE. SEE SOON.

Fun & Games

Look at the illustrations and put the letter on each next to the numbered words. Try hard to remember as many as you can before looking them up on previous pages.

1. name _____
2. live _____
3. goodbye _____
4. hello _____
5. Deaf _____
6. hearing _____
7. sign _____
8. London _____
9. many_____
10. town_____
11. where_____
12. what_____
13. little_____
14. Sheffield_____

a.

b.

c.

g.

d.

h.

e.

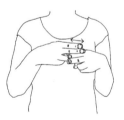

i.

f.

j.

k.

m.

l.

n.

Chapter 4

Knowing Me, Knowing You

. . . .

In This Chapter

▶ Why it is not rude to point

▶ Talking about friends and family

▶ Asking for and giving information about work and colleagues

▶ Describing workplaces

. . . .

*W*hen people meet, they usually start off after greetings with questions such as 'How's life?', 'How's work?', 'How's your family?', and so on. They then go on to chat about other things. This chapter shows you how to conduct a conversation about your family, friends, and work colleagues.

Don't Point! It's Rude! Or Is It?

You may have been told when you were a child that it was rude to point and you may feel uncomfortable doing it, but for BSL users pointing is necessary, not rude!

Pointing is used a lot for *referencing* in BSL, to identify people or objects specifically and to place them in space or time. When a signer indicates a location for a person or object, she can subsequently use pointing to refer to the person or object again without mentioning names or having to repeat the signs already given. You can also use pointing to introduce a new person or object in a different location and can refer to them again by pointing to where they were first established.

In addition, you can use pointing to refer to people or things that are not present.

Telling Others about Yourself

This section helps you to give, ask for, understand and share information about yourself, family, and friends. It gives you most everyday signs related to work and home.

Family and friends

Talking about your family is a good way to start a conversation. Memorising the signs for family members in Table 4-1 will help you.

Table 4-1		Family Members	
English	**Sign**	**English**	**Sign**
MOTHER		FATHER	
SISTER		BROTHER	
DAUGHTER		SON	
AUNT/ NIECE or UNCLE/ NEPHEW		FAMILY	

English	Sign	English	Sign
COUSIN		PARTNER	
DIVORCED		MARRIED/ HUSBAND/ WIFE	
CHILDREN			

If you want to sign **parents,** just sign **mother/father**.

In BSL, you don't sign 'and' and little words such as 'the', 'an', and 'to'.

Signs for **grandmother, grandfather,** and **grandchildren** are easy to sign as you need only fingerspell 'G' before using the sign for **mother, father, children, son,** and **daughter.**

If you want to crack a joke about your **mother-in-law**, just sign **mother** then spell L-A-W. Likewise for **father-in-law**, and **parents-in-law**. In other words, you don't sign the 'in'.

What about **stepmother**, **stepfather**, **stepsister**, and **stepbrother**? Fingerspell S-T-E-P then sign the person.

Again, what about **half sister** or **half brother**? Sign **half,** then sign **brother** or **sister**.

Want to practise a few signs? Here are some examples for you to try:

English: Is she your mother?
Sign: YOUR MOTHER?

English: No. She's my aunt.
Sign: [head shake] MY AUNT

English: She is my half sister
Sign: MY HALF-SISTER

You now know the signs for family, but what about your friends?

Table 4-2 gives you the signs you need to know so you won't make the mistake of introducing your school friend as your mother.

Table 4-2		Friends	
English	*Sign*	*English*	*Sign*
PEOPLE		MAN	
WOMAN		GIRL	
BOY		FRIEND	

Try this example:

English: All the people here are women.
Sign: PEOPLE HERE ALL WOMAN

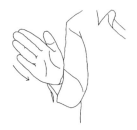

Talking about your job

In this section, you can start asking for and giving information about your work and colleagues. Be careful when talking about confidential aspects of your job: BSL users have sharp eyes and can watch your signing from a distance.

Many non-BSL users don't realise that signing can be seen and understood from a long distance (useful in a disco) so be careful if you want to slag off the boss.

The signs in Table 4-3 are related to occupations.

Table 4-3		Jobs	
English	*Sign*	*English*	*Sign*
TEACHER		DOCTOR	
NURSE		POLICE OFFICER	

English	Sign	English	Sign
SHOP ASSISTANT		MANAGER/ BOSS	
INTERPRETER		DRIVER	
SECRETARY		ADMIN-ISTRATOR	
MECHANIC		WAITER/ WAITRESS	
SOLICITOR		SOCIAL WORKER	

(continued)

Table 4-3 *(continued)*

English	Sign	English	Sign
DENTIST		STUDENT	

Discussing your workplace

When talking about your work, you need to know signs for workplaces. Check out Table 4-4 for common workplaces.

Table 4-4 — **Workplaces**

English	Sign	English	Sign
SHOP		FACTORY	
SCHOOL		COLLEGE	

English	Sign	English	Sign
OFFICE		STATION	
HOSPITAL		GARAGE	

Starting to Sign

Old school friends, Peter and Mark, chat about their family and work.

Peter:	Are you still a schoolteacher?
Sign:	YOU STILL TEACHER SCHOOL?

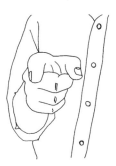 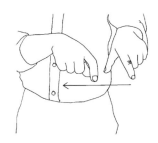

 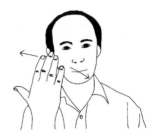

Mark: No, I'm an office manager now. What about you?
Sign: [head shake] ME OFFICE MANAGER NOW. YOU?

Peter:	I'm working as a BSL interpreter in an office.
Sign:	ME WORK B-S-L INTERPRETER OFFICE

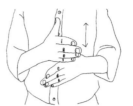

Mark:	Your friend, Mary, was a nurse?
Sign:	YOUR FRIEND M-A-R-Y BEFORE WORK NURSE, RIGHT?

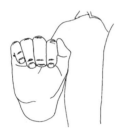

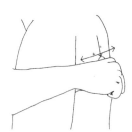

Peter: No, she's a doctor in a hospital now.
Sign: (head shake and pointing) DOCTOR HOSPITAL NOW

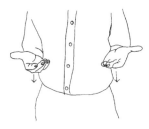

Mark: How's your son?
Sign: YOUR SON OK?

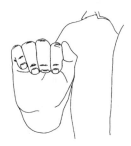

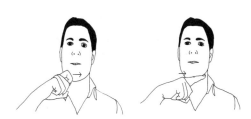

Peter: Fine, he is a dental student at college.
Sign: (Head nod) F-I-N-E DENTIST STUDENT COLLEGE NOW

Fun & Games

Try to match the occupation signs with their workplaces and see how many you can remember without peeping at the illustrations in this chapter!

1. SHOP

2. SCHOOL

3. HOSPITAL

4. FACTORY

5. OFFICE

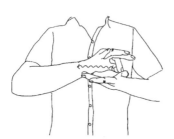

6. GARAGE

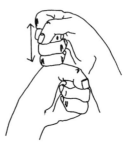

7. COLLEGE

8. STATION

a. DOCTOR

b. MECHANIC

c. ASSISTANT

d. ADMINISTRATOR

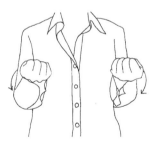

e. BUS DRIVER

f. SECRETARY

g. TEACHER

h. MANAGER

If you manage to succeed in matching the signs, try to do the following exercises yourself, or even better, practise with a friend. If your occupation is not in the list, don't worry, just pick one that is and pretend!

1. Describe your family.

2. Sign what you do and where you work.

● ●

Chapter 5

Expressing Your Feelings

· ·

In This Chapter

▶ Showing feelings

▶ Talking about how you feel

▶ Describing a pain in your body

▶ Signs for emergencies

· ·

*W*alking along a road, you see a couple of Deaf people signing and one is grimacing as if in pain. Don't send for an ambulance, he is probably only describing something that happened to someone he knows. Sign language is an expressive medium (think opera 'diva') and signers show their feelings, rather than describe them.

In this chapter you discover useful medical signs that will help in an emergency where you need to communicate with a Deaf BSL user.

How's Life? Talking about Your Feelings

In spoken language you indicate the intensity of your feelings by the tone of your voice, for example, when using words such as 'happy', 'furious' or 'bored'. You can emphasise the feeling by adding an adverb or adjective to show the degree of feeling, for example, 'very happy', 'absolutely furious', and 'really bored'. In BSL, a signer shows the deeper feeling by using a more emphatic facial expression.

Not only does a signer's face indicate his feelings but it also conveys other significant information about how something is done. Different expressions can give different meanings to the same sign. An example is 'walk', as it can be modified with facial expressions, possibly allied to a gesture or body language, to show how a person is walking, that is, 'walking slowly', 'walking fast', 'walking angrily', and 'walking happily'.

Have a look at the examples below for different meanings of 'walk'.

Walking happily   **Walking angrily**

Be careful with your expressions (especially when meeting a prospective mother-in-Law) as you can easily give a wrong meaning.

In BSL, you sign 'I' and 'me' the same way. Just point to yourself with your index finger and don't mouth the words.

Take a look at Table 5-1 for examples of feelings:

Table 5-1		Feelings	
English	*Sign*	*English*	*Sign*
HAPPY		SAD	

English	Sign	English	Sign
DEPRESSED		ANGRY	
EXCITED		DISAPPOINTED	
PLEASED		NERVOUS	
FED UP		FRIGHTENED/ ANGRY	

(continued)

Table 5-1 (continued)

English	Sign
MISERABLE	

Starting to Sign

 Jill is talking to Tom in the works canteen and she notices that he is looking depressed.

Jill: Why are you looking miserable?
Sign: YOU MISERABLE WHY

Tom: I'm fed up with work.
Sign: ME FED UP WORK

Jill: Why is that? I'm happy here.
Sign: WHY? ME HAPPY HERE

Tom:	I'm angry and depressed because my boss has told me I have to work more hours.
Sign:	ME ANGRY DEPRESSED. BOSS TOLD ME HAVE TO WORK MORE HOURS

You OK? Talking about your health

Feeling rotten or feeling great? If you're talking to a friend about how you're feeling use this sign for **feel**.

If you sign thumb up (**good**) after **feel**, it means 'feel good' and if you use clenched fist with your little finger up(**bad**) after **feel**, it means 'feel bad'.

The signs in Table 5-2 help you to describe your symptoms to your friend.

Table 5-2		Symptoms	
English	*Sign*	*English*	*Sign*
ROTTEN		SICK/ NAUSEA	
SICK/ VOMIT		HEADACHE	
PAIN/HURT		DIZZY	

English	Sign	English	Sign
COLD		COUGH	
TEMPERATURE		ILL/ POORLY/ SICK	
BRUISE		BROKEN	

Knowing a few medical signs does not mean you can interpret for a Deaf person. A mistake, however small, can affect a diagnosis and have serious consequences. Interpreting in a medical situation must ALWAYS be done by a fully qualified sign language interpreter if possible.

The following phrases would come in handy when describing your ailments to a friend or interpreter.

English: I feel rotten and have nausea.
Sign: FEEL ROTTEN NAUSEA

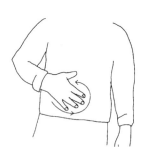

English: I feel dizzy and have a headache.
Sign: ME DIZZY HEADACHE

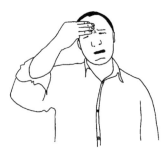

English: I have a pain and have been sick.
Sign: ME PAIN BEEN SICK

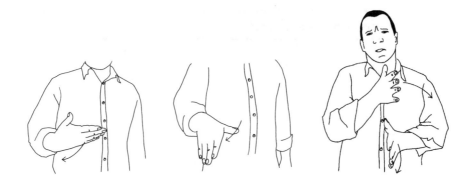

Where does it hurt?

You may be describing a pain to a friend who may ask where the pain is. Table 5-3 gives you the words and signs for body parts. You usually sign them by pointing to or touching that particular part.

Table 5-3	Where on Body?		
English	**Sign**	**English**	**Sign**
ARM		HAND	
BODY		BACK	

(continued)

Table 5-3 *(continued)*

English	Sign	English	Sign
LEG		FOOT/ FEET	
STOMACH		CHEST	

Table 5-4 gives you the signs linked to the head. Again, you indicate these by pointing to or touching the feature.

Table 5-4   **Where on Head?**

English	Sign	English	Sign
HEAD		EYE	

English	Sign	English	Sign
EAR		NOSE	
MOUTH		THROAT	
TEETH		JAW	

People with arthritis, or joints making funny noises, should find the signs in Table 5-5 useful for describing where the pain is.

Table 5-5		Creaking Joints	
English	**Sign**	**English**	**Sign**
ANKLE		ELBOW	
HIP		KNEE	
NECK		WRIST	

If you are feeling poorly, these phrases may get you sympathy from your friends, if not they do not understand the signs or they are a hard-hearted bunch.

English: My throat hurts.
Sign: MY THROAT HURT

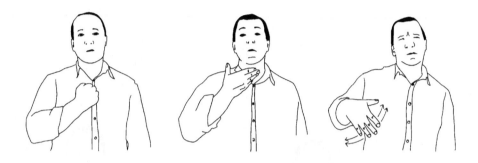

English: I have a pain in my back.
Sign: MY BACK PAIN

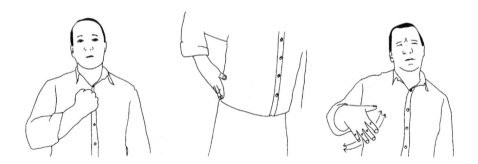

English: I have a bad cold and cough.
Sign: ME BAD COLD COUGH

English: My neck is really painful.
Sign: (pointing) NECK BAD PAIN

Just take one of these

A doctor may use the signs in Table 5-6 to explain what treatment you need.

Table 5-6		Medical Procedures	
English	*Sign*	*English*	*Sign*
BANDAGE		SUTURE/ STITCH	
INJECTION		BLOOD	
TEST/EXAMINE		BLOOD PRESSURE	
OPERATION/ SURGERY		DRUGS	

An operation can be on any part of the body. Therefore, when describing a particular operation, the sign is made on the part of the body to be operated on. You sign stitches/sutures by miming the sewing where the operation was, or is to be, performed.

Try the following phrases for practice.

English: I am afraid of injections and stitches.
Sign: ME AFRAID INJECTION STITCHES

English: My blood pressure is high.
Sign: MY BLOOD PRESSURE HIGH

English: I'm having an operation on my hip.
Sign: ME HIP OPERATION

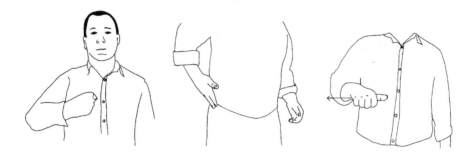

English: Do you think my arm is broken?
Sign: YOU THINK ARM BROKEN

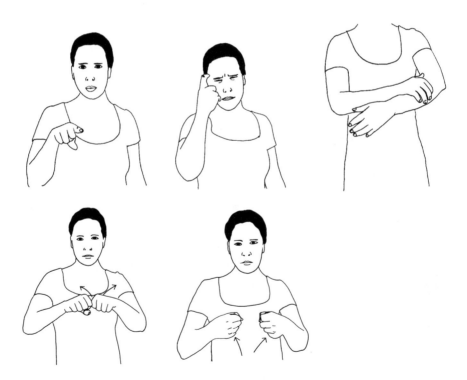

999 Emergency

In an emergency, the signs in Table 5-7 can save someone's life.

Table 5-7		Useful Signs for Emergency	
English	*Sign*	*English*	*Sign*
EMERGENCY		AMBULANCE	
HOSPITAL		HEART ATTACK	
BLEEDING/ HAEMORRHAGE		SUSPECTED	

The sign for **bleeding/haemorrhage** is the same as **blood**, fast repetitions of the sign indicate heavier bleeding.

Starting to Sign

 Olga, who is hearing, is concerned about Peter who does not look very well.

Peter: I have a pain in my chest and arm.
Sign: ME PAIN ARM CHEST

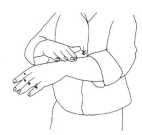 

Olga: I think you may be having a heart attack.
Sign: ME THINK YOU HEART ATTACK

Peter: My doctor told me my blood pressure is high.
Sign: DOCTOR TOLD [ME] BLOOD PRESSURE HIGH

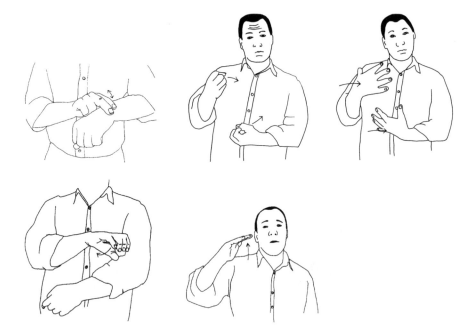

Olga: I'll ring 999 and ask for ambulance.
Sign: ME RING 999 CALL AMBULANCE

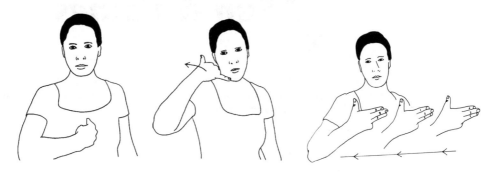

Fun & Games

The statements and questions numbered 1–7 below are ones that a doctor may use or ask. Look at the illustrations and see whether you can work out which one goes with each statement or question.

1. Do you have a cough?

2. Do you feel sick?

3. I'd better bandage that.

4. Your blood pressure is high.

5. Do you have a headache?

6. That cut on your leg is bleeding.

7. Something broken?

a.

b.

c.

d.

e.

f.

g.

Chapter 6

Nailing Numbers

. . . .

In This Chapter

▶ Looking at regional variations

▶ Signing numbers

▶ Signing time and age

▶ Signing how much

. . . .

*I*n no area of Sign Language do we notice regional variations in signs as much as with numbers. In this chapter, we look at numbers used in London and the south of England, but you need to be aware that other areas may have different signs. We also give you the low-down on how to explain what time it is, how old you are, and how much you just spent in the sales.

Explaining Regional Signs

In this chapter, we look at the regional variations in signs then at the signs for numbers. Hopefully this number overview can help you to nail the numbers signs.

Deaf people use different signs for the same word in different areas of the UK. We call these differences *regional variations*. Though people in a particular area use the signs in general use in that area, they can usually understand the regional signs used in other areas, in the same way that a person living in the South uses 'little' and 'baby' themselves but readily understands the words 'wee' and 'bairn', as used in Scotland.

To take a general example, you sign **people** in different ways depending on where you're from. BSL users in Hull, Birmingham, and London respectively use the following signs for **people**.

PEOPLE (Hull)   **PEOPLE** (Birmingham)   **PEOPLE** (London)

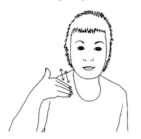      

 If you see a sign you do not understand or recognise, do not panic! Just say sorry and ask for clarification. Deaf BSL users may not always understand regional signs so they have to check unfamiliar regional signs in the same way a hearing listener would, if speaking to someone who had a broad Scots, Scouse, or Geordie dialect.

Numbers? Count me in

Do you count on your fingers? People naturally use their fingers to count. In a crowded and noisy pub, you may put up your hand showing four fingers to indicate you want four pints. When you do so, would you stop to think what you were doing before counting and holding up the four fingers? No, it would just come naturally. You do the same for BSL numbers signs. The signs for one to ten are easy to master.

See below for some examples of different regional variations. In order, you can see the sign used for **ten** in London, Birmingham, and Manchester.

TEN used in London.   **TEN** used in Birmingham.   **TEN** used in Manchester.

You use the sign shown here with finger wiggling movement for **how many?**

HOW MANY?

The illustrations here show numbers one to ten .

Table 6-1		Numbers 1–10	
English	**Sign**	**English**	**Sign**
ONE		TWO	
THREE		FOUR	

(continued)

Table 6-1 *(continued)*

English	Sign	English	Sign
FIVE		SIX	
SEVEN		EIGHT	
NINE		TEN	

Now you know the signs for one to ten, you can give your phone number to that gorgeous person you may have your eye on. Now let's see whether you can memorise 11 to 20.

Table 6-2 gives you numbers 11 to 20.

Table 6-2		Numbers 11–20	
English	**Sign**	**English**	**Sign**
ELEVEN		TWELVE	
THIRTEEN		FOURTEEN	
FIFTEEN		SIXTEEN	
SEVENTEEN		EIGHTEEN	
NINETEEN		TWENTY	

Note that you sign the 'teen' signs the same as one to nine but add a few back and forth sideways movements. When signing two-figure numbers from **20–99**, you move your hand slightly to the right after making the first number, changing to the second number as it moves. The following illustrations show this movement:

TWENTY THREE

FORTY SIX

FIFTY ONE

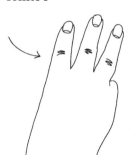

 For decade numbers such as **30**, **40**, **50**, and so on, all you need to do is to sign the first number, then move it outwards. These examples give you a better understanding:

THIRTY   **SEVENTY**   **EIGHTY**

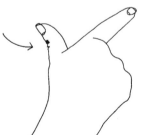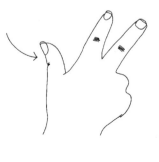

For three-figure numbers, you've two different ways of counting, for example, for **126** the first way is to move your fingers slightly sideways as you sign the numbers. The other way is to sign **100** and then **26**, as shown in these examples:

126 [ONE-TWO-SIX]

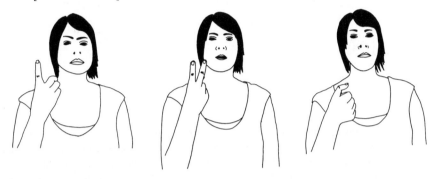

126 [ONE HUNDRED TWENTY-SIX]

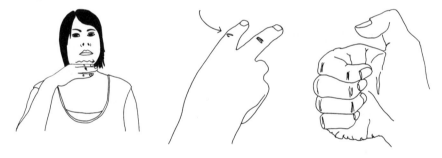

Hundred, **thousand**, **million**, and **billion** have their own signs. You can sign any number you need using these signs.

HUNDRED

THOUSAND

MILLION

BILLION

You may think that you've now mastered the signs for numbers but you haven't finished yet as you've different ways of signing numbers when talking about age, money, and time. Don't fret, we give more examples. Soon you will be able to discuss the ages of your friends (discreetly, of course), discuss prices, and ask for and give times.

Who's first?

Imagine that you've won first prize in a raffle – a BMW convertible. Naturally you want to tell your friends about your good luck, but how do you sign it? BSL has a specific hand movement to indicate ordinal numbers – a twisting of your wrist inward while signing the number, as the examples below show.

FIRST

SECOND

FIFTH

SEVENTH

Telling the time

You know the signs for numbers but how do you sign time? Say you want to arrange a time to meet your friends at the pub. As in English, hours in the day are divided into 'o'clock', 'past', and 'to' in phrases such as 'one o'clock, 'ten past two', 'half past four', 'a quarter to three'. Note in the illustrations in this section that you use a special movement to show the hour, for example, one o'clock. This movement is the same as for the ordinal numbers.

TIME?

PAST

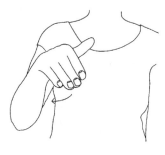

TEN PAST TWO

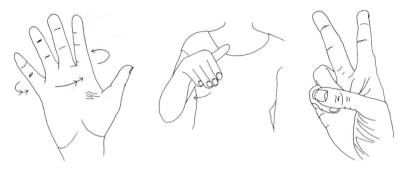

FIVE TO THREE

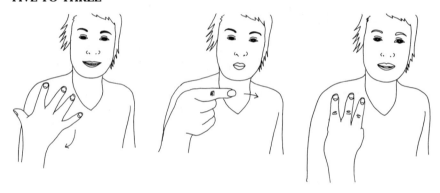

ONE O'CLOCK

EIGHT O'CLOCK

When signing half past the hour, you do not use the **past** sign, you just sign, for example, **half five** even if you still mouth 'past'.

In BSL to show the difference between a.m. and p.m., you sign **morning**, **afternoon,** or **night** after the number.

THREE O'CLOCK MORNING

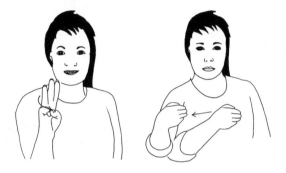

HALF PAST FOUR AFTERNOON

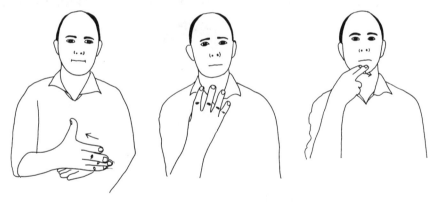

When telling time, BSL users do not usually use the digital system of times for example, for 8:40 they sign **twenty to nine**; for 16:25 it would be **twenty-five past four**.

Talking about money

Some people try to avoid telling their partners how much they've spent on clothes except when they bought them in a sale. If you've bought something at a bargain price, you may want to tell your partner how much it cost. So how do you do sign (with a smug look on your face) 'guess how much this cost . . . ?' The sign **how much** shown here is the same as the sign for **how many** but you sign it on the chin instead.

HOW MUCH?

To show pounds sterling, the number sign starts at the chin and moves forward, but from £13 onwards, you sign the pound symbol as **L** on the palm of a hand. Pence is signed as **p**.

POUND   **TWO POUNDS**   **EIGHT POUNDS**

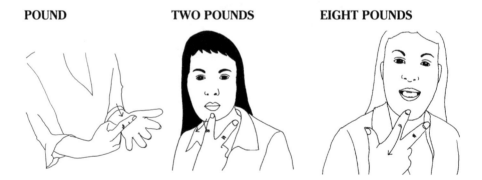

FIFTY-FIVE POUNDS

TWENTY PENCE

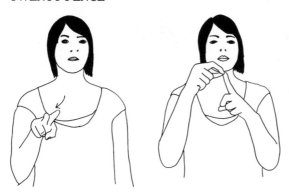

Asking someone's age

Ask people their age with caution! If you really have to ask someone for their age or give yours (for example, to say 'of course I'm over 18' when buying alcohol) you use the same sign for **how many** and **how much** but start the sign on the nose.

HOW OLD   **FOUR YEARS OLD**

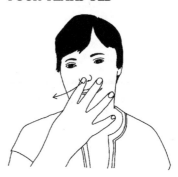

The hand movement for decade numbers and two-figure numbers is forward instead of sideways.

FORTY YEARS OLD

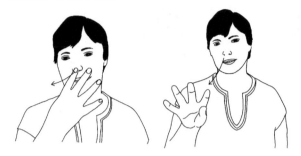

THIRTY TWO YEARS OLD

Signin' the Sign

 Olga is having coffee with Jean. Olga is talking about her brother's birthday.

Olga: It's John's birthday next week
Sign: John BIRTHDAY NEXT WEEK

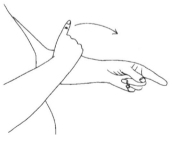

Jean: How old will John be?
Sign: John HOW OLD?

Olga: He'll be forty.
Sign: FORTY

Jean: When is his birthday?
Sign: BIRTHDAY WHEN?

Olga: It's on May 3rd.
Sign: M-A-Y 3RD

Jean: What have you bought for his birthday?
Sign: YOU BUY WHAT?

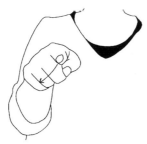

Olga: I bought him three shirts.
Sign: BOUGHT 3 SHIRT

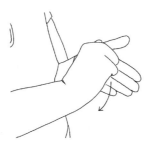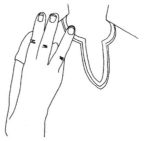

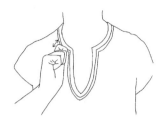

Jean: I'm nosey! How much were the shirts?
Sign: ME NOSEY! SHIRT HOW MUCH?

Olga: I bought two for £34 and got one free!
Sign: BOUGHT 2 £34. ONE FREE

   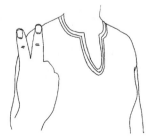

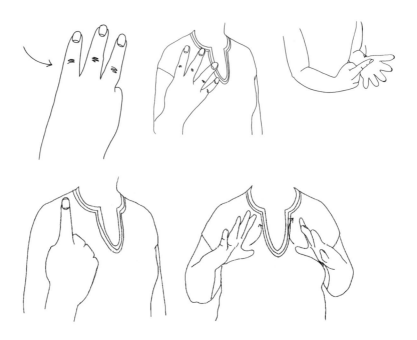

Jean:	What time is the party starting?
Sign:	PARTY START WHAT TIME?

Olga: It'll start at 8.30.
Sign: START HALF PAST EIGHT

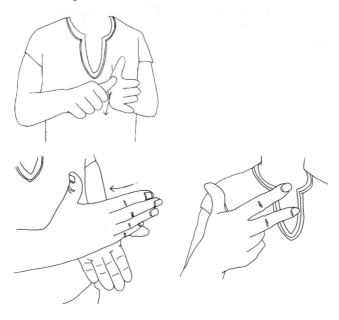

Fun & Games

Look at the illustrations and see whether you can remember the signs.

1.

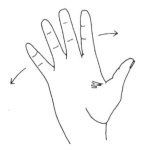

2.

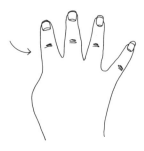 

3.

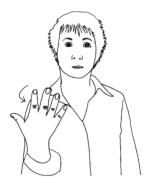

4.

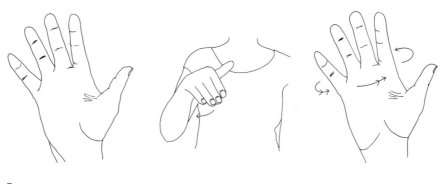

5.

6.

7.

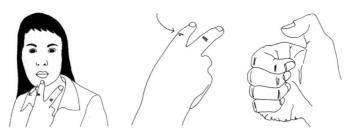

8.

9.

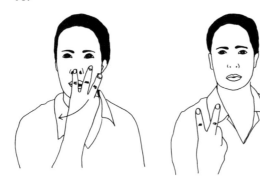

10.

If you remember the signs, try to sign these questions to yourself and also sign the answers. Even better, practise with a friend.

Remember to sign the answers after signing the questions.

1. CAR NUMBER?

2. DOOR NUMBER?

3. HOUSE NUMBER?

4. PHONE NUMBER?

5. HOW OLD?

6. MY SHIRT HOW MUCH?

7. BIRTHDAY WHEN?

8. NOW WHAT TIME?

Chapter 7

Describing Weather, Colour, and Clothes

*B*ritish people talk more about the weather than any other topic, and who can blame them? This chapter looks at the signs used to describe the weather and the clothes we may wear to match it. Talking about clothes also gives us a chance to talk about colour, so this chapter introduces you to some basic signs to help you brighten up your BSL conversation.

Signing Come Rain, Come Shine

The topic of the weather is an excellent icebreaker and you can use it to fill in lulls in the conversation. The signs in Table 7-1 give you a good vocabulary that enables you to have a good moan with a Deaf person.

Table 7-1		Weather		
English	**Sign**		**English**	**Sign**
RAIN			SNOW	
WET			DRY	
WIND/Y			FOG/ FOGGY	
SUN(NY)			CLOUDY	

English	Sign	English	Sign
HOT		COLD	
WARM		FROST/ FREEZING	

If you're stuck at home on a rainy day, practise these signs and drive the gloom away.

English: It's cold, raining, and wet today.
Sign: TODAY COLD RAIN WET

TODAY

COLD

RAIN

WET

English: It is snowing and freezing outside.
Sign: OUTSIDE SNOW FREEZE

English: Tomorrow it will be foggy.
Sign: TOMORROW FOGGY

English: It will be hot, sunny, and dry next week.
Sign: NEXT WEEK HOT SUNNY DRY

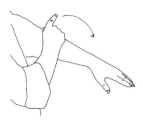 

was windy and cloudy but warm yesterday.
ESTERDAY WINDY CLOUDY WARM

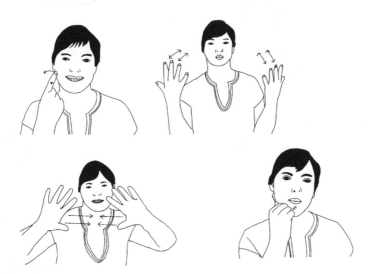

Describing Colours

Colour brightens our lives and knowing the signs for colours can add colour
to your conversation. The signs for colours often come from things that
are usually that colour, such as lips/**red**, grass/**green**, **blue**/veins on hands,
white/collar, **black**/black face of a miner, **pink**/colour of skin, and **yellow**/
blond hair.

Table 7-2 shows you how to sign the basic signs for colours.

Table 7-2		Colours	
English	*Sign*	*English*	*Sign*
WHITE	Or	BLACK	
BLUE		GREEN	
RED		YELLOW	
ORANGE		BROWN	

English	Sign	English	Sign
PINK		GREY	
PURPLE		FAVOURITE	

Now you have the signs for colours it would be useful to find out the signs for clothes so you can surprise your partner by paying them a compliment on their dress sense. The next section gives you the signs for clothes.

Developing Dress Sense

Describing what clothes' you've got on today is a typical area of descriptive signing. The sign for **clothes** is the same for **wear** but you sign it twice.

WEAR

CLOTHES

Eyeing up everyday clothes

Be careful how you describe your partner's new dress to a friend of hers,
a black and purple summer dress would not be a good description if it was
actually green and white. Use the signs in Table 7-3 to make sure that does
not happen.

Table 7-3	Everyday Clothes		
English	*Sign*	*English*	*Sign*
DRESS		SKIRT	
TROUSERS/ JEANS		BLOUSE	
JACKET		TIE	

English	Sign	English	Sign
SHOES		SLIPPERS	

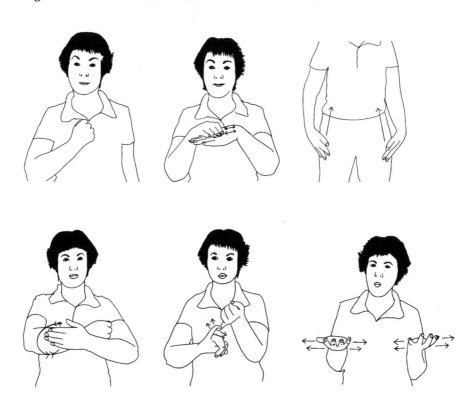

Try these sentences for size.

English: Where are my blue trousers and brown shoes?
Sign: MY BLUE TROUSERS BROWN SHOES WHERE?

English: I'm wearing my white jeans and yellow blouse.
Sign: ME WEAR WHITE JEANS YELLOW BLOUSE

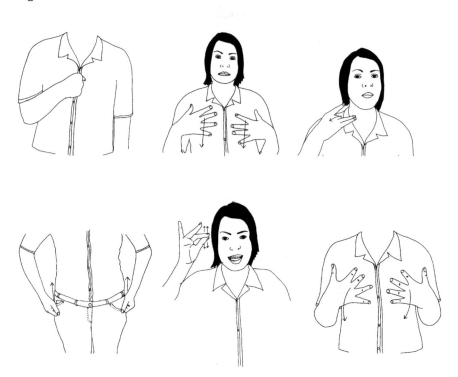

English: I like dresses and skirts.
Sign: ME LIKE DRESSES SKIRTS

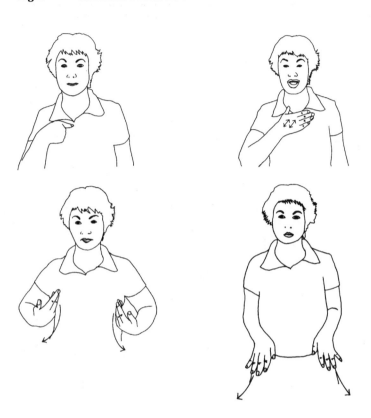

Mentioning the unmentionables

What about the clothes we wear that we don't reveal in public. For items that we wear under our clothes, have a look in Table 7-4. You sign some items in a way that represents how you put them on. For example, you sign **pants** (for both men and women) the same way. How would you describe Bridget Jones' knickers? Just give the size as you give the sign.

Table 7-4		Items of Underwear	
English	*Sign*	*English*	*Sign*
PANTS		BRIEFS	
KNICKERS		BRA	
TIGHTS		T-SHIRT	

Wrapping up winter warmth

Winter means putting on extra clothes for warmth. The signs in Table 7-5 show you what they are.

Table 7-5		Warm Clothes	
English	**Sign**	**English**	**Sign**
VEST		JUMPER/ SWEATER	
HAT		SCARF	
COAT		BOOTS	
SOCKS		GLOVES	

You can remember **hat, scarf** and **gloves** signs easily. You just sign them as if you're putting them on.

You sign **boots** like the action of pulling them on to your legs but the sign is at arms length, below waist level.

Here is some practice for you:

English: Where are my hat and coat?
Sign: MY HAT COAT WHERE?

English: Don't forget your jumper, scarf, and gloves.
Sign: [head shakes] FORGET JUMPER SCARF GLOVES

English: Are the black boots yours?
Sign: BLACK BOOTS YOURS?

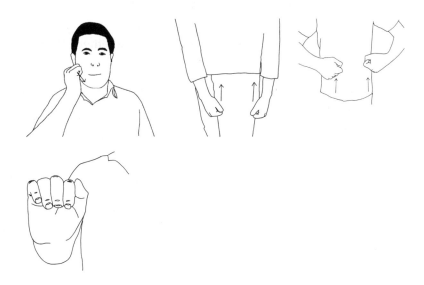

English: I can't find my red socks.
Sign: (head shakes) CAN'T FIND RED SOCKS

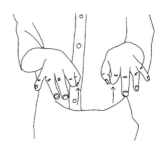

Putting a spring in your signs

Spring is when you stop wearing your winter clothes and prepare to face the rain. The signs in Table 7-6 enable you to check whether a Deaf friend is well prepared.

Table 7-6		Spring	
English	*Sign*	*English*	*Sign*
UMBRELLA		RAINCOAT	

Try signing the things that keep you dry:

English: Where is my umbrella?
Sign: MY UMBRELLA WHERE?

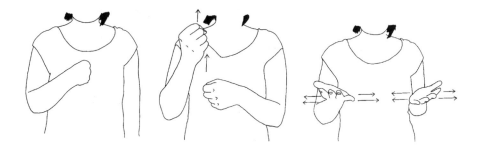

English: Where are my raincoat and boots?
Sign: MY RAINCOAT BOOTS WHERE?

Summer sun (if you're lucky)

Everyone needs to get their wardrobe sorted for Summer, particularly if you happen to be jetting off to the sun. Table 7–7 gives you some handy signs to describe your holiday packing.

Table 7-7		Beach Wear	
English	*Sign*	*English*	*Sign*
SWIMWEAR		BIKINI	
SHORTS		SWIMMING TRUNKS	

The sign for sunglasses is the same for glasses but you sign **sun** before **glasses**. Swimwear comes in different sizes and colours, and you use your hands to describe what they look like. A **bikini** is signed the same as **bra** and **pants**.

Starting to Sign

Mark and Peter are going on holiday and they discuss what to pack.

Mark: I'm taking three pairs of shorts.
Sign: ME BRING THREE SHORTS

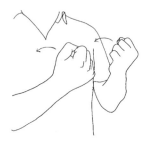

 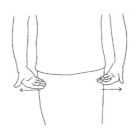

Peter:	I'm taking five T-shirts.
Sign:	ME TAKE FIVE T-SHIRTS

 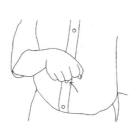 

Mark:	How many swimming trunks are you bringing?
Sign:	YOU BRING HOW MANY SWIMMING TRUNKS

 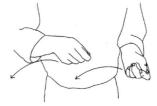

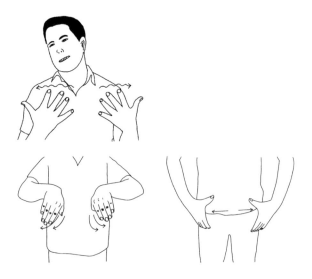

Peter: Only one. Don't forget to pack a jumper.
Sign: ONE. [head shakes] FORGET PACK JUMPER

If you mix these colours, what colour do you get? Make the sign!

1. Red and yellow make . . .

2. Blue and yellow make . . .

3. Black and white make . . .

4. Red and white make . . .

5. Red and blue make . . .

6. Red and green make . . .

Imagine you're packing a suitcase for your holiday. Try to remember the signs for the items you want to take before you check on previous pages.

Part III
Getting Out and About

The 5th Wave   By Rich Tennant

"I'm all for being patient around the British Sign Language learning curve, but I'm pretty sure he's trying to tell us it's raining."

In this part . . .

Want to arrange to meet Deaf friends for a drink, make a date, find your way about the place, or order food in a restaurant? This Part's for you.

From telling the time to giving complicated directions, everything's here to help to make yourself understood when getting out and around with Deaf people.

Chapter 8

Getting from A to B

*T*his is a chapter about space and place, and we start by describing the most important space of all to a signer: The space around them in which they make their signs. We also discuss the wheres and whys of prepositions.

The practical signs in this chapter may help you to be a good Samaritan and give directions to a Deaf person who is lost. They'll also give you a chance to plan social outings with Deaf friends, and talk about local landmarks when you're out and about.

Signing Space

BSL is a visual language. Signers produce signs with one or two hands in space in front of and around their bodies, from above the top of the head to just below the waist. The space they use is called the *signing space*. To help you visualise this space, imagine an invisible photo frame around yourself, no more than arm's length in all directions.

Signing space

The described signing space may seem too large an area for your eyes to follow all the signs and movements within it but you do not need to. If you focus on the signers face, which in itself gives a lot of visual information, you can still see the signs in your peripheral vision.

As a new signer, your eyes are naturally drawn to the signer's moving hands and you may miss important information shown on the signer's face and lips. Resist this tendency and try to concentrate on the face, though you will need time and practise to be able to do so effectively.

Placement of signs

Placement is the act of establishing people, objects, buildings, and anything else within the signing space so that you can refer back to that thing by just pointing to where you originally placed them. This placement of things is a bit like referring to somebody by name, then subsequently referring to them as 'she' or 'he'.

Prepositions

In English language, prepositions are words to describe where someone or something is — for example 'on', 'in', 'under', 'beside', 'next', 'behind', and so on. For example, in English, you can say 'The man is standing next to the woman', 'The cup is on the saucer', and 'The book is under table'. In BSL, signs for prepositions do exist but BSL also uses signs to show the EXACT location. For example, you would indicate 'The book is under the table' with one hand placed palm down in front of you and the other hand, representing the book, being placed under the first one. You can even show the book standing on end, instead of lying flat, by turning the hand upright instead of flat. Here is an example:

English: The book is under the table.
Sign: TABLE BOOK UNDER

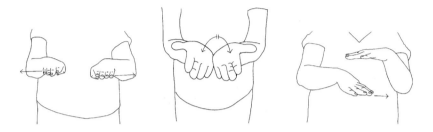

How Do I Get To . . .?

Before you acquire the signs for outside locations, landmarks, and directions, you need to familiarise yourself with those used in buildings. Many of these signs can also be also be used outside.

Table 8-1 gives basic directions on how to sign, well, basic directions.

Table 8-1		Basic Directions		
English	*Sign*		*English*	*Sign*
LEFT			RIGHT	
UPSTAIRS			DOWN-STAIRS	

(continued)

Table 8-1 *(continued)*

English	Sign	English	Sign
NEXT		OPPOSITE	
STRAIGHT		BESIDE	
FLOOR		TOILETS	
WINDOW		DOOR	

Take a look at the following sentences and see how you can use these basic signs to give simple directions.

English: The men's toilets are upstairs on the second floor.
Sign: MEN TOILET UPSTAIRS SECOND FLOOR

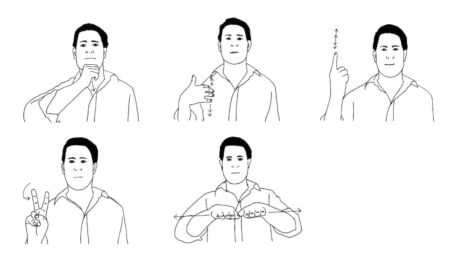

English: The lift is straight on, next to the green door.
Sign: LIFT STRAIGHT GREEN DOOR NEXT

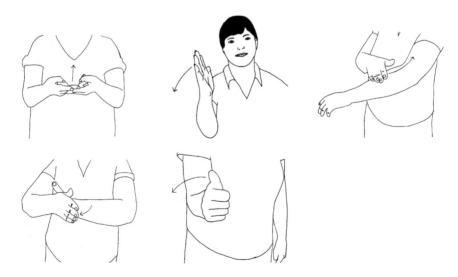

English: The stairs are opposite the lift.
Sign: LIFT OPPOSITE STAIRS

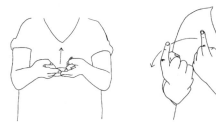

Getting to and from work

Whether you walk or use public transport to get to work, the signs shown in Table 8-2 come in handy when describing how you get there, or to other places.

Table 8-2		Modes of Transport		
English	**Sign**		**English**	**Sign**
CAR			BUS	
TRAIN			TAXI	

English	Sign	English	Sign
WALK		BICYCLE	
MOTOR-CYCLE		FERRY	
UNDER-GROUND/TUBE		TRAM	

To sign **car**, you mime holding a steering wheel and turn your hands as if steering. You do the same for **bus**, **van** or **lorry** but mime a bigger steering wheel.

Because of regional variations, the sign for **bus** differs in different places in the UK. Among older people in London, **bus** is signed as if they were pulling the line inside the bus that used to tell the driver that someone wanted to get off at the next stop.

BUS

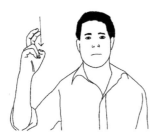

Practise the sentences below to see if you can remember the different types of transport.

English: I get to work by bus and train.
Sign: GET TO WORK BUS TRAIN

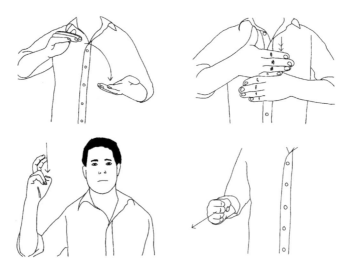

English: I used to go to work by car but now go by bicycle.
Sign: BEFORE GO WORK CAR NOW BICYCLE

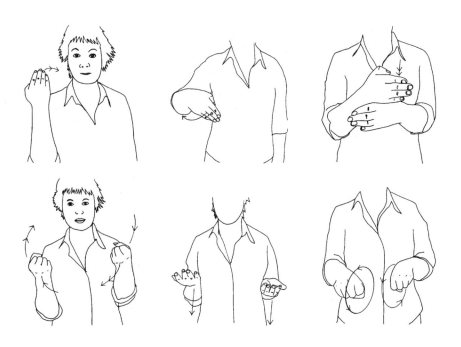

English: There are too many people on the underground so I go by tram.
Sign: UNDERGROUND TOO MANY PEOPLE ME GO TRAM

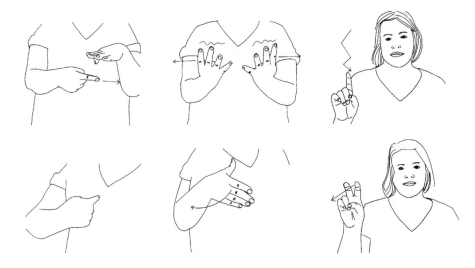

In BSL, the sign **get to** is the same as **arrive**.

Location, location, location

You may confuse somebody when giving directions if you don't use the correct signs. The signs below enable you to direct somebody to the right location.

Familiarise yourself with the signs for north, south, **east,** and west, all you have to do is to move your hand towards the different points of the compass.

NORTH   SOUTH   WEST

EAST

When someone signs to you, their 'east' is towards your left – which would be towards YOUR 'west', that is, east and west are reversed because you're facing in opposite directions. When signing 'north-east', 'south-west', and so on, you sign the north or south first, and then the other sign.

English: I live in North London.
Sign: ME LIVE NORTH LONDON

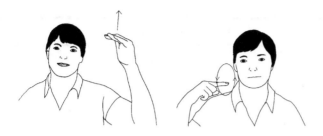

English:	I work in the South-West.
Sign:	ME WORK SOUTH WEST

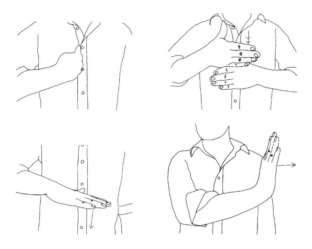

Looking out for local landmarks

Deaf people use landmarks a lot when giving directions in BSL. Rather than directions such as 'follow the A23 through the town until you get to the B3404, turn left there, and the Church is 100 yards on the left', you would sign something like 'follow A23 through town, under railway bridge, first left after cricket ground, church down there on left'.

Table 8-3 gives you the signs you may use to give directions in a town.

Table 8-3		Local Landmarks	
English	*Sign*	*English*	*Sign*
ROAD		BRIDGE	
POSTBOX		TRAFFIC LIGHTS	
CORNER		ROUND CORNER	
T-JUNCTION		CROSS ROADS	
MOTOR-WAY		POST OFFICE	

To indicate a road sign, you use both index fingers to draw a square shape or one index finger to draw a circle in the air, depending on its shape.

Now you're familiar with basic directions, see if you can sign the following sentences:

English: Drive along the road until you reach traffic lights, turn left.
Sign: ME ROAD DRIVE TRAFFIC LIGHTS LEFT

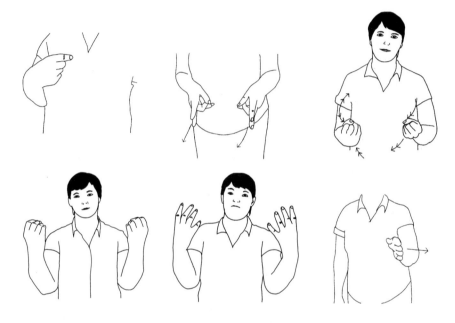

English: The post office is on the corner of the T-junction.
Sign: T-JUNCTION POST OFFICE THERE

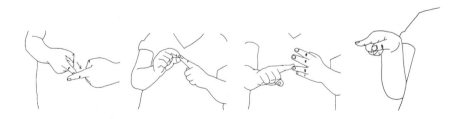

You can show the exact corner by placing your upright hands at right angles to each other.

English: The post box is round the corner on the left.
Sign: ROUND CORNER LEFT POST BOX

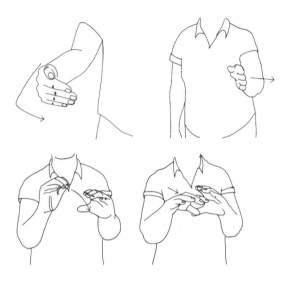

English: Turn right at the crossroads and the motorway is straight on.
Sign: CROSSROADS RIGHT STRAIGHT MOTORWAY

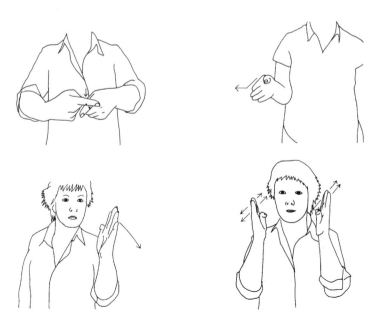

Countryside landmarks

Using landmarks to give directions is helpful as most can be easily spotted. Table 8-4 gives you the signs.

Table 8-4	Landmarks in the Country		
English	**Sign**	**English**	**Sign**
FARM		WINDMILL	
RIVER		LAKE	
TOWER		HILL	

(continued)

Table 8-4 *(continued)*

English	Sign	English	Sign
TREE		CANAL	

The sign for **forest** is the same as for **tree** but is signed several times (how many times depends on the size of the forest) with the hand moving to the right and rotating as it moves along.

English: The forest is on the hill.
Sign: HILL FOREST

English: Turn right after the lake.
Sign: LAKE RIGHT

 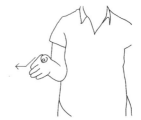

English: The farm is on the other side of the river.
Sign: RIVER OVER FARM THERE

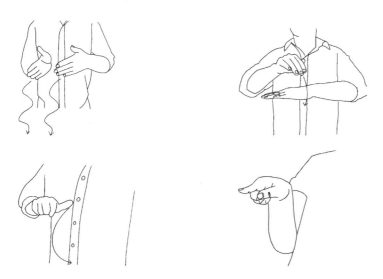

Out on the Town

Before you can arrange to meet Deaf friends in town you need to acquire the signs in Table 8-5.

Table 8-5	Local Places		
English	*Sign*	*English*	*Sign*
RESTAURANT		PUBLIC HOUSE (PUB)	

(continued)

Table 8-5 *(continued)*

English	Sign	English	Sign
CINEMA		THEATRE	
SUPERMARKET		GARAGE	
PARK		MUSEUM	

Do you feel ready to paint the town red with these signs? Try these phrases:

English: She went to a restaurant, then the cinema.
Sign: SHE GO RESTAURANT GO CINEMA

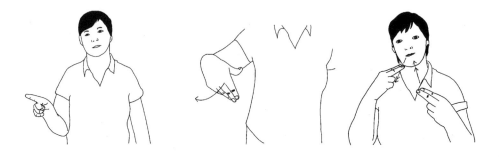

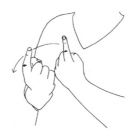

English: The museum is opposite the theatre.
Sign: MUSEUM OPPOSITE THEATRE

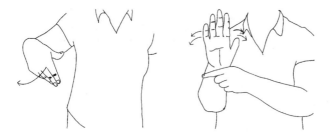

English: I want to go to the supermarket next to the garage.
Sign: ME WANT GO SUPERMARKET NEXT GARAGE

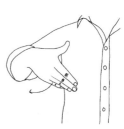

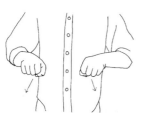

Starting to Sign

Jean is arranging a night out in town with her friend Paul.

Jean: Where do you want to go? Pub?
Sign: (eyebrows raised) GO WHERE? PUB?

 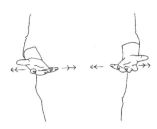

Paul: What about the cinema?
Sign: CINEMA? (querying expression)

Jean: Where is the cinema?
Sign: CINEMA WHERE?

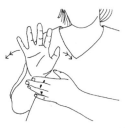 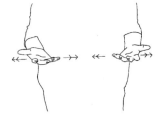

Paul: Go over the bridge, past the park to the traffic lights, turn left. Cinema is on the right.
Sign: OVER BRIDGE PAST PARK TRAFFIC LIGHTS LEFT CINEMA RIGHT

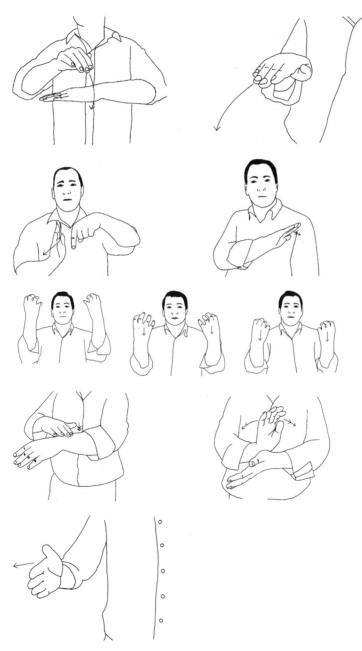

Jean: I remember now, it is opposite the pub.
Sign: (head nodding) REMEMBER NOW OPPOSITE PUB

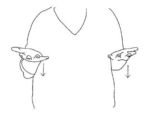
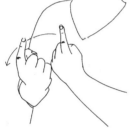

Sign the following words. Look back in the chapter for help if you need to but first try to remember the signs independently.

1. Sign four different modes of transport.   (worth 4 points)

2. Sign three different landmarks in the country.   (worth 3 points)

3. Sign two different buildings in town.   (worth 2 points)

4. Sign the words 'traffic lights' and 'bridge'.   (worth 2 points)

5. Sign the words 'T-junction' and 'crossroads'.   (worth 2 points)

6. Sign the words 'canal' and 'windmill'.   (worth 2 points)

A total of fifteen points is possible. How did you get on?

11-15: You won't get lost!

6-10: You need help but you'll get there eventually.

1-5: You'd better stay at home and keep practising!

Chapter 9

Arranging Not So Blind Dates

*1*t's time to talk about time. This chapter helps you to make someone's day by giving you the signs that enable you to arrange meetings with them. We also talk through signs for days and months, and special holidays and celebrations.

On the grammar side of things, we cover the use of tenses in BSL so you can talk about past and future events.

Getting Tense about Time

BSL has no tenses as you find in English and other languages. Instead it has markers that show past, present, and future. These markers are called *timelines* and they refer not to just past, present and future but periods of time over hours, weeks, months, and years. Two commonly used timelines are:

Timeline A: The shoulder is used for reference to times in the past – for example: **before**, **recently**, and **previous.** You sign all these words backwards from the shoulder.

BEFORE

The sign for **before** can be used as the basic sign for many other related signs such as **past**, **recent**, **previous**, **not long ago**, **a long time ago**, and **ages ago**. You show the difference between these signs by the use of facial expressions and, usually, repetitive movements in conjunction with the sign .

PAST

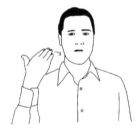

RECENT

For the future, signs are forward from the cheek or chest area and as the time moves further into the future, you make the signs further away from the body.

FUTURE

EVERY DAY

Timeline B: the arm and hand are used to indicate shorter time periods such as **weekly**, **next week**, **last week**, **every week**, **monthly**, **regularly**, **usually**. The illustrations below show how the direction of movement gives specific meanings.

NEXT WEEK   **LAST WEEK**

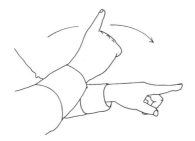

Arranging to Meet

Fancy meeting a Deaf friend for a quick drink, a bite to eat, or to see a film? You'll probably have more fun if you both turn up on the right day and at the right time. This section shows you how to do just that.

Today's the day

This section gives you the days of the week so you won't make a mistake when arranging to meet a deaf friend. See Table 9-1 for the signs for each day of the week and related vocabulary.

Table 9-1		Days of the Week		
English	**Sign**		**English**	**Sign**
SUNDAY			MONDAY	

(continued)

Table 9-1 *(continued)*

English	Sign	English	Sign
TUESDAY		WEDNESDAY	
THURSDAY		FRIDAY	
SATURDAY		THIS WEEK	
LAST WEEK		NEXT WEEK	

English	Sign	English	Sign
MORNING		AFTERNOON	
EVENING		NIGHT	

You make the signs for **Monday**, **Tuesday**, and **Wednesday** the same way as the signs for the alphabets **M**, **T**, and **W** but you spell the letters twice.

Be careful when signing **Friday**. The sign is similar to the sign for **Father** but you sign **Friday** with the dominant forefinger and index finger making a circular movement (anti-clockwise) on the passive forefinger and index finger of the other hand. The sign for **Sunday** is the same as for **prayer** but you bring the hands together twice.

English: Meet on Sunday? (with a querying look)
Sign: MEET SUNDAY?

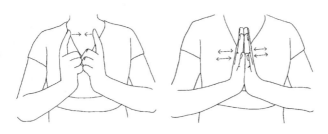

English: See you Wednesday evening.
Sign: SEE YOU WEDNESDAY EVENING

When shall we meet?

When your Deaf friend signs **Let's meet again** the signs in Table 9-2 help you to get the right date in your diary. It would not do for you to leave your friend standing outside the cinema on the wrong day.

Table 9-2		Dates	
English	*Sign*	*English*	*Sign*
TODAY		TOMORROW	

English	Sign	English	Sign
YESTERDAY		DAY	
WEEK		WEEKEND	
MONTH		YEAR	

In the south of the UK, especially among older people, **yesterday** is signed for ward from the cheek instead of backwards – see the next illustration.

YESTERDAY

English: Are you here next week?
Sign: YOU HERE NEXT WEEK?

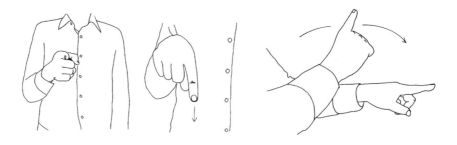

 If you sign **week** rapidly forwards and backwards in a flat circular movement, it indicates **every week**. You sign **week after week** with a slow forward and backward movement and, in most cases, a resigned expression, to indicate **boredom**. You can add a number to the sign to show the number of weeks involved such as **two weeks ago**, every **three weeks,** and **in four weeks**.

English: When are you having your holiday this year?
Sign: YOU HOLIDAY THIS YEAR WHEN?

Starting to Sign

 Jean and Olga are arranging to meet for coffee.

Olga:	Want to meet for coffee? Tomorrow?
Sign:	WANT MEET COFFEE. TOMORROW?

Jean:	No, I'm working tomorrow. How about Tuesday evening?
Sign:	(head shake) ME WORK TOMORROW. TUESDAY EVENING?

Olga:	Sorry, I can't, as I'm meeting my friend. What about Saturday morning?
Sign:	SORRY CAN'T, ME MEET FRIEND. SATURDAY MORNING?

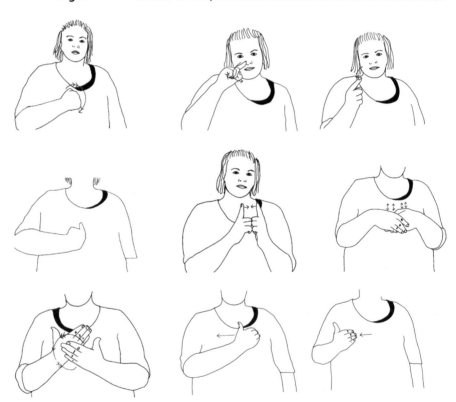

Jean: No, how about next Monday?
Sign: (head shake) NEXT WEEK MONDAY?

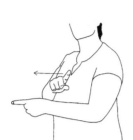

Olga: Monday is fine. Morning or afternoon?
Sign: MONDAY FINE. MORNING AFTERNOON?

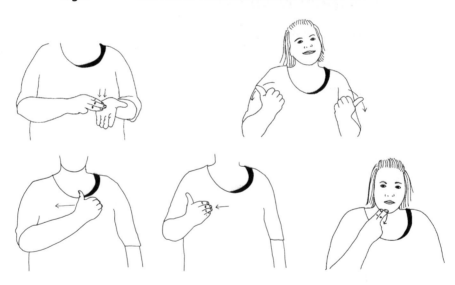

Jean:	Afternoon is fine.
Sign:	AFTERNOON FINE

Mastering months

So what about months? They're quite easy as you only finger-spell the first three letters of the month. Some letters, however, you skip – see below for finger-spelled examples:

JANUARY: J-A-N

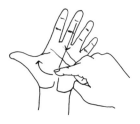 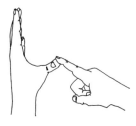 

FEBRUARY: F-E-B

 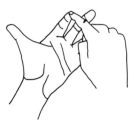 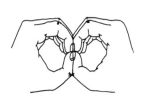

MARCH: M-C-H

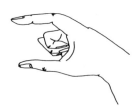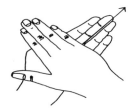

MAY: M-A-Y

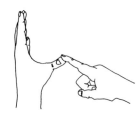

JUNE: J-N-E

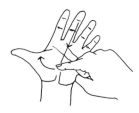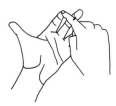

JULY: J-L-Y

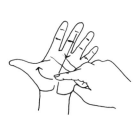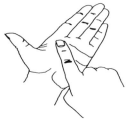

AUGUST: A-U-G

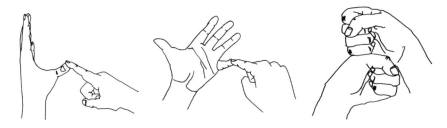

SEPTEMBER: S-E-P-T

OCTOBER: O-C-T

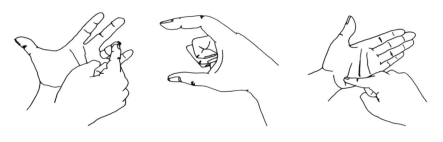

NOVEMBER: N-O-V

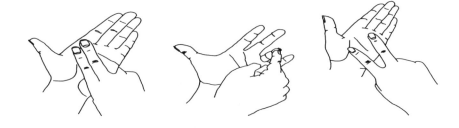

DECEMBER: D-E-C

You may say 'Hang on, April is missing!'. This month is not forgotten! **April** is the only month of which only the first letter is finger-spelled. You spell A but spell it twice quickly.

In some regions, signs for months exist, many of them originating from residential schools for Deaf children. One example, from the Jewish Residential School (now closed), is **March**, illustrated here:

MARCH

Special Celebrations

We can't end the chapter without mentioning the special days we celebrate throughout the year. The signs in Table 9-3 show these:

Table 9-3		Special Celebrations	
English	**Sign**	**English**	**Sign**
CELEBRATE/ PARTY		NEW YEAR	
EASTER		CHRISTMAS	
BANK HOLIDAY			
DIVALI		PASSOVER	
RAMADAN			

English: It's Christmas next month.
Sign: CHRISTMAS NEXT MONTH

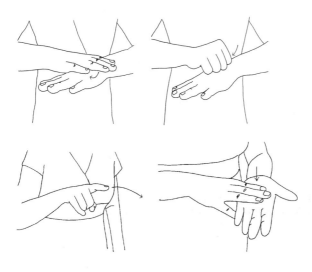

English: He will celebrate the Jewish New Year next week.
Sign: (pointing) NEXT WEEK CELEBRATE JEWISH NEW YEAR

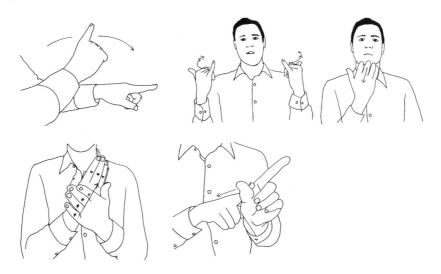

English: Happy Easter!
Sign: HAPPY EASTER

English: We celebrated Christmas last week.
Sign: LAST WEEK WE CELEBRATE CHRISTMAS

 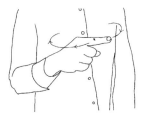

Fun & Games

Look at the illustrations and see whether you can remember the signs. The answers are in Appendix A.

1.

2.

3.

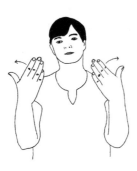

4.

5.

6.

7.

8.

9.

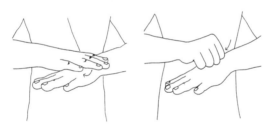

10.

If you managed to remember the signs, here is another activity. On the next page is a diary for the coming week and you have to tell your friend what you're doing every day. Alternatively, practise with a friend, taking it in turns to suggest a possible day and time to meet for a coffee.

Sunday	**Thursday**
11:00: Coffee with Jason	10:15: Meet Tony
p.m.: Work in garden	p.m.: Work
7:00: Dinner with Amelia	
Monday	**Friday**
12:30: Lunch with Mum	p.m.: Shopping
7:00–9:00: BSL class	Eve: Pub with Jem and Andy
Tuesday	**Saturday**
a.m.: Work	p.m.: Tennis with Mark
6:30 p.m.: see Doctor	Eve: Party
Wednesday	
Emma's birthday – 21 today	
p.m.: Swimming	

Chapter 10

Fancy Fish and Chips?

*W*hen dining in or eating out with your Deaf friends, they may ask you what you would like to have, what you would like to order from the menu, which wine you prefer or just discuss food generally. The signs in this chapter enable you to talk turkey, chat about cheese, or waffle on about wine.

On Today's Menu

These days people eat out with friends a lot or invite each other for dinner. A Deaf friend might ask you to stay overnight, or even for the weekend. Knowing the signs for food and tableware helps you to survive without any major mishaps.

Which knife and fork to use?

When having a meal, you may want to ask for a missing knife or fork or for someone to pass the salt. Acquiring the signs below in Table 10-1 may spare you the embarrassment of having to eat with your fingers or eat unseasoned food.

Table 10-1		Tableware	
English	**Sign**	**English**	**Sign**
KNIFE		FORK	
SPOON		PLATE	
CUP		MUG	
WINE GLASS		NAPKIN	
SALT		PEPPER	

These few sentences prepare you to ask for items you may need:

English: Pass me the plate please
Sign: PASS PLATE PLEASE

English: Which do you want – cup or mug?
Sign: CUP MUG WHICH?

English: Sorry, I have no fork.
Sign: SORRY NO FORK ME

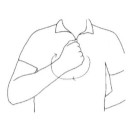

You sign **breakfast**, **lunch**, **eat**, and **food** the same way, it should be easy to lipread the actual word:

The sign for dinner is different:

Want breakfast?

Staggering downstairs half awake in the morning, you need to know the sign for **coffee**. Table 10-2 shows the signs you need for breakfast.

Table 10-2		Breakfast	
English	*Sign*	*English*	*Sign*
COFFEE		TEA	
MILK		SUGAR	
CEREAL		BACON	
EGG		SAUSAGE	

(continued)

Table 10-2 *(continued)*

English	*Sign*	*English*	*Sign*
BREAD		BUTTER/ MARGARINE	
JAM		MARMALADE	
CROISSANT		TOAST	

You see from these illustrations that some of the signs mimic the actions involved. You sign **cup** and **mug** how you hold them when drinking; milk is derived from milking a cow; the signs for **bacon** and **croissant** show their shapes; **toast** comes from the action of putting the bread in the toaster. Now check out the following signs:

English: Do you want bacon, egg, and sausage?
Sign: YOU WANT BACON EGG SAUSSAGE?

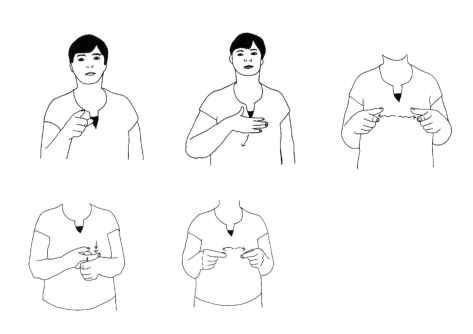

English: Which would you like: croissant, toast or plain bread?
Sign: CROISSANT TOAST PLAIN BREAD WHICH?

English: Would you like tea or coffee? With milk and sugar?
Sign: TEA COFFEE MILK SUGAR?

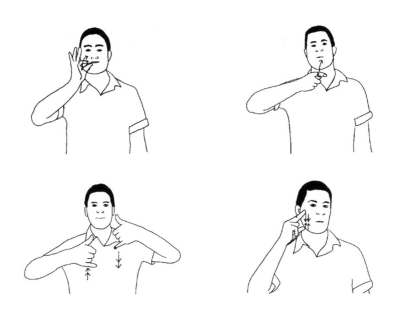

English: Can I have the butter and jam please?
Sign: BUTTER JAM PLEASE?

Raise your eyebrows when using YES/NO questions. You don't have to sign 'want' for tea or coffee.

Grabbing a quick lunch

If grabbing a quick lunch with your Deaf colleagues at work, the signs in Table 10-3 can help you to discuss what to have. Be careful with your hand shapes or you may end up with a croissant instead of a roll.

Table 10-3		Lunch	
English	*Sign*	*English*	*Sign*
SANDWICH		HAM	
CHEESE		CHICKEN	
SALAD		ROLL	

(continued)

Table 10-3 *(continued)*

English	Sign	English	Sign
CHIPS/FRIES		SOUP	
CRISPS		JACKET POTATO	

Now try signing these examples:

English: I want a ham and salad sandwich please
Sign: ME WANT HAM SALAD SANDWICH PLEASE

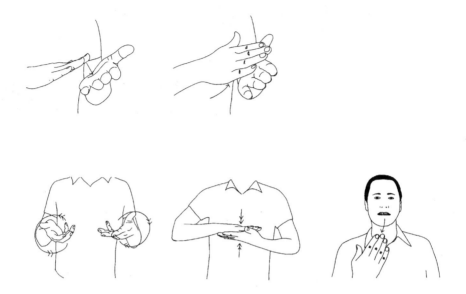

English: What do you want? Chicken and chips?
Sign: YOU WANT WHAT? CHICKEN CHIPS?

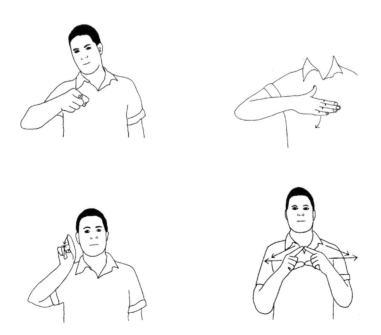

English: I'd like to have soup, a roll, and crisps.
Sign: ME WANT SOUP ROLL CRISPS

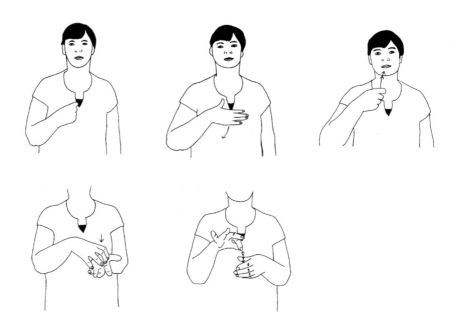

English: I don't know which to have – a cheese roll or a jacket potato.
Sign: ME DON'T KNOW WHICH CHEESE ROLL JACKET POTATO

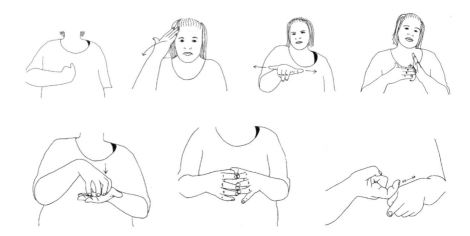

Starting to Sign

 Mark is popping down to the cafe to get lunch and asks his colleagues what they want.

Mark: I'm going to the cafe. Anything you want?
Sign: ME GO CAFE. YOU WANT?

Jean: I want two bacon rolls and coffee with milk.
Sign: ME WANT TWO BACON ROLL COFFEE MILK

John: I'd like to have toasted sandwiches with sausage.
Sign: ME WANT TOASTED SAUSAGE SANDWICH

Olga: Jacket potato with cheese for me please.
Sign: JACKET POTATO CHEESE PLEASE

Peter: Chicken soup, crisps, and tea.
Sign: CHICKEN SOUP CRISPS TEA

James: I want fish and chips.
Sign: WANT FISH CHIPS

 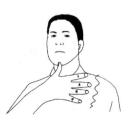 

Tea, a drink with jam and bread

Everyone knows the British for their tea breaks: Tea is culturally important to them. To discover all the possible signs you may need, you can take afternoon tea with a refined Deaf lady pensioner, but the signs in Table 10-4 give you what you need to order what you want for tea.

Table 10-4		Afternoon Tea	
English	*Sign*	*English*	*Sign*
CUCUMBER		TOMATO	
BISCUIT		CAKE	
SCONE		CREAM	
CHOCOLATE		FRUIT	

Prepare to stuff yourself with cucumber sandwiches and scones with cream after memorising these signs!

English: I love scones with cream and jam!
Sign: ME LOVE SCONE CREAM JAM

English: Which would you like, fruit or chocolate cake?
Sign: WANT FRUIT CHOCOLATE CAKE WHICH?

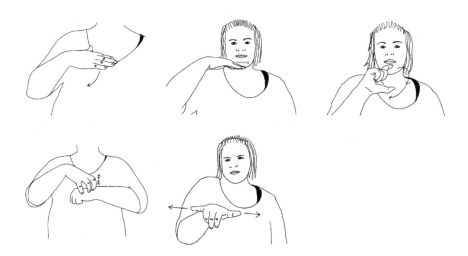

English: I'd like cucumber sandwiches, chocolate biscuits, and tea.
Sign: WANT CUCUMBER SANDWICH CHOCOLATE BISCUIT TEA

What's for dinner?

Meat, potatoes, and vegetables used to be the staple meal of the British public but choices have now widened to include foods from other countries. (For more food signs, take a look at the later section 'Eating Out'). If you feel hungry at the thought, put your mind to the signs in Table 10-5.

Table 10-5		Dinner	
English	*Sign*	*English*	*Sign*
MEAT		LAMB	
PORK		ROAST	
FISH		VEGETABLES	
POTATOES		CHOPS	
PIE		BAKED BEANS	

You sign **meat**, **lamb**, and **pork** the same as for **beef**, **sheep**, and **pig** respectively.

English: We're having fish pie and vegetables.
Sign: WE HAVE FISH PIE VEGETABLES

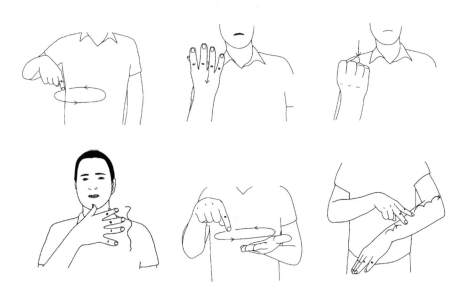

English: Pork chops with potatoes and baked beans.
Sign: PORK CHOPS POTATOES BAKED BEANS

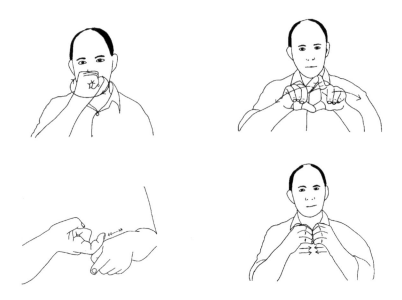

Having a couple of glasses of wine may help you to relax and express your-self without inhibition – though whether anyone understands you is another matter. Don't overdo it though or you may get the signs wrong and end up with the dog's dinner.

Eating Out

The UK has so many sorts of restaurant to choose from now and you may have to ring up to book a table. For more on arranging to go out see Chapter 8. The signs in Table 10-6 help you to tell your Deaf friends you've reserved a table in a restaurant.

Table 10-6	Useful Signs for Eating Out		
English	*Sign*	*English*	*Sign*
RESTAURANT		TABLE	
RESERVATION		FOREIGN	

Deaf people prefer to eat at a round table as doing so enables them to see each other clearly when talking. When making a reservation, try to reserve a round table. Also remove any vases, candles, lamps, and so on, from the middle of the table as they block the diners view of each other.

Do not to speak with food in your mouth, your fellow diners have no wish to see the progress of the food you've been chewing. Lip patterns are an impor-tant part of BSL and you won't be able to speak clearly if you have your mouth full. The same applies to chewing gum.

Take-away food

Deaf people enjoy eating ethnic food and curry is now one of the most popular dishes, even beating fish and chips. Other ethnic foods are equally popular. The signs in Table 10-6 help you to discuss with your Deaf friends what their favourites are.

Table 10-6		Take-away Food	
English	**Sign**	**English**	**Sign**
CHINESE		SWEET AND SOUR	
ITALIAN		PIZZA	
INDIAN		CURRY	
PASTA		RICE	

English	*Sign*
BURGER	

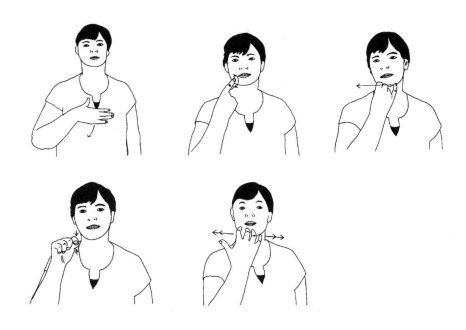

English: I'd like to have sweet and sour chicken with rice.
Sign: WANT SWEET SOUR CHICKEN RICE

English: I like pizza and pasta.
Sign: ME LIKE PIZZA PASTA

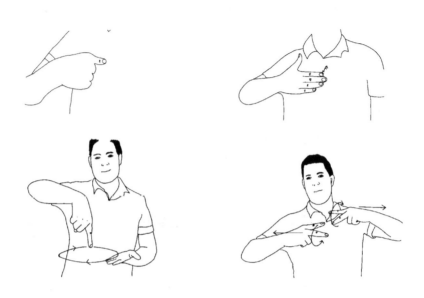

English: Do you want fish and chips? With curry sauce?
Sign: YOU WANT FISH CHIPS CURRY SAUCE

Fancy a drink anyone?

Whether you're down the pub, selecting an aperitif at a dinner party, or ordering from a wine menu, it's always useful to be able to describe what you're having to a Deaf friend.

English: I would like a glass of red wine.
Sign: ME LIKE GLASS RED WINE

English: A bottle of white wine please.
Sign: BOTTLE WHITE WINE PLEASE

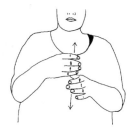 

Fun & Games

How about trying to order from the menu below? You can look back in the chapter for help, but try hard first.

MENU

1. Vegetable soup

2. Tomato soup

3. Lamb chops, potatoes, and vegetables

4. Chicken curry and rice

5. Jacket potato with cheese and salad

6. Cheese and tomato pizza

7. Fish and chips

8. Toasted ham and tomato sandwich and crisps

9. Two scones with cream and jam

10. Chocolate cake

11. Fruit pie

12. Mug of coffee

13. Tea and biscuits

Chapter 11

Making the Most of Your Free Time

*I*n this chapter, we cover signs for various activities, sports, and hobbies. These signs enable you to ask Deaf friends about their leisure activities and give you a sporting chance of understanding their replies.

Having Fun with Leisure Activities

If you like outdoor activities, Table 11-1 gives you the signs for activities that you can enjoy by yourself or with friends.

Table 11-1		Leisure Activities	
English	*Sign*	*English*	*Sign*
INTEREST/HOBBY		HORSE RIDING	

(continued)

Table 11-1 (continued)

English	Sign	English	Sign
SIGHTSEEING		WALKING	
CLIMBING		FISHING/ANGLING	
CAMPING		SAILING	
CYCLING		HIKING/RAMBLING	

In English, activities have 'ing' at the end of words such as camping, sailing, and so on. In BSL, you don't use the 'ing' so you mouth the words as 'camp' and 'sail'.

Signin' the Sign

 Mark asks his work colleagues what they are doing in the summer.

Mark:	What will you do this summer?
Sign:	THIS SUMMER YOU DO?

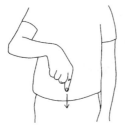 

John:	I'm going cycling and sightseeing.
Sign:	ME CYCLING SIGHTSEEING

Peter: I'm going on a walking and climbing holiday.
Sign: ME WALK CLIMB HOLIDAY

Olga: I'm going riding and camping.
Sign: ME RIDE CAMP

James: I like fishing and sailing.
Sign: ME LIKE FISH SAIL

Jean: I will go on a rambling holiday with my partner.
Sign: ME GO RAMBLING HOLIDAY WITH PARTNER

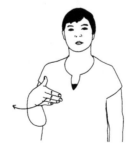
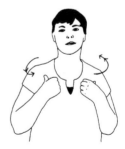

Getting Sporty

Kick off by memorising these signs so you can discuss or argue about sports with Deaf friends. You sign most sports by the way in which you would hold and use the equipment. For example, the sign for **badminton** is holding the racquet and miming hitting a shuttlecock with it, using only your wrist, while tennis would show someone serving, with a bigger arm action.

This tip helps you to remember the signs. Try this activity after looking at Table 11-2. Find a stick, ruler, or similar and use it to mime the action of sports activities such as **tennis**, **golf**, and **cricket**. Do them all with the stick to get the feel of them, then repeat them without the stick. Signing sports is as simple as that! The sign for **rugby** would be how you do an underhand pass to a team mate. For **squash** the action would be at a lower level than tennis.

Table 11-2 gives the signs for sporting activities.

Table 11-2		Sports Activities	
English	*Sign*	*English*	*Sign*
TENNIS		FOOTBALL	
GOLF		HOCKEY	

English	Sign	English	Sign
CRICKET		RUGBY	
BADMINTON		SQUASH	
SWIMMING		SKIING	
SKATING		BOXING	

You sign ball by using your hands to show the size and shape. You can show a small ball (golf/squash) on one hand, larger ones with two.

Practise the following sentences:

English: You like sports?
Sign: YOU LIKE SPORTS?

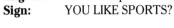

English: I love golf and tennis.
Sign: ME LOVE GOLF TENNIS

English: I go swimming after playing squash.
Sign: ME GO SWIM AFTER SQUASH

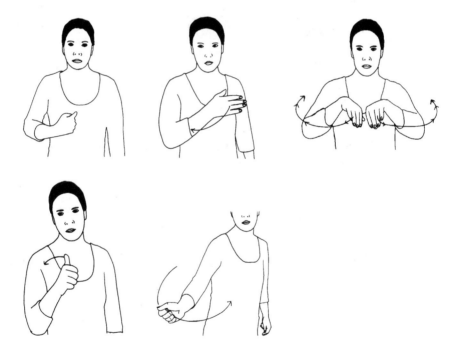

Equip yourself with the signs in Table 11-3 and you won't be stumped if some-one asks you for sports results.

Table 11-3		Sports Results Words	
English	*Sign*	*English*	*Sign*
MATCH/TOURNAMENT		TEAM	
RACE		SCORE	
REFEREE/ UMPIRE		WIN/WON	
LOSE/LOST		DRAW	

You sign **referee** or **umpire** the same way, by putting thumb and forefinger near your lips as if you're holding a whistle and blowing it.

Likewise, you sign **match** and **tournament** the same way, but repeat the sign several times, in a downward direction, for tournament – denoting a number of matches being played.

Count is signed just like **Score** but using one hand only.

Starting to Sign

 Mark and Peter discuss sports.

Mark:	Are you playing football tomorrow?
Sign:	TOMORROW YOU PLAY FOOTBALL?

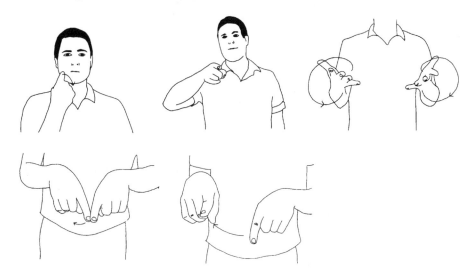

| **Peter:** | No, I'm playing in a badminton match. What about you? |
| **Sign:** | (head shake) NO ME PLAY BADMINTON MATCH. YOU? |

| **Mark:** | I'm watching the cricket match in the afternoon. |
| **Sign:** | AFTERNOON ME WATCH CRICKET MATCH |

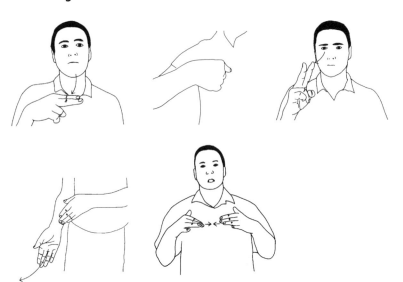

Peter: I'm watching rugby on Sunday.
Sign: SUNDAY ME WATCH RUGBY

Mark: Do you like watching boxing?
Sign: YOU LIKE WATCH BOXING?

Peter: No, I prefer to watch skiing.
Sign: (head shake) ME PREFER WATCH SKIING

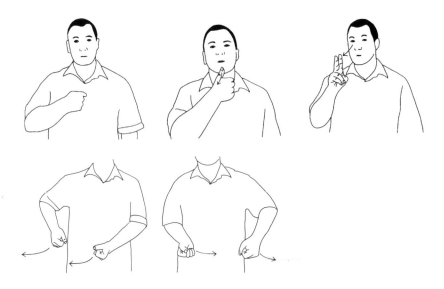

Playing Indoor Games

Find out the signs for indoor games and you have winning hands. Most Deaf Clubs have strong indoor games sections where members play whist, darts, dominoes, draughts, chess, snooker, pool, and table tennis, and compete in club competitions or against other clubs.

Table 11-4 gives the signs for indoor games:

Table 11-4	Indoor Games		
English	**Sign**	**English**	**Sign**
CARDS		CHESS	
DRAUGHTS		DOMINOES	
DARTS		SCRABBLE	
SNOOKER		COMPUTER GAMES	

The sign for **cards** is miming dealing the cards. For any card game, you finger-spell the name, then sign **cards**. For example, for whist, you fingerspell W-H-I-S-T, then give the sign. Alternatively, some Deaf people mouth the word 'whist' while signing **cards**. For more on fingerspelling, refer to Chapter 2.

The sign for **dice** is miming shaking the dice in your hand and throwing them.

English: I play chess and draughts.
Sign: ME PLAY CHESS DRAUGHTS

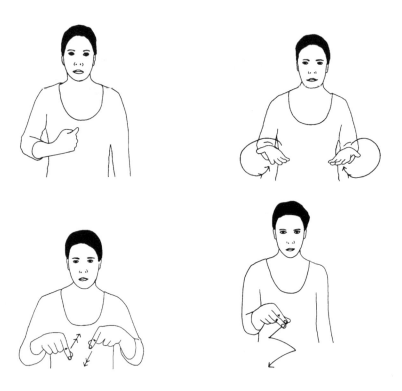

English: I play cards and darts with friends.
Sign: ME PLAY CARDS DARTS WITH FRIENDS

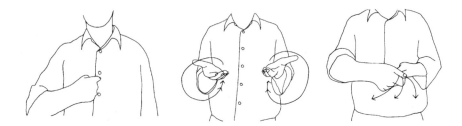

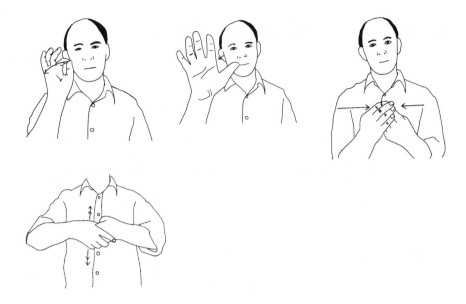

English: You like playing computer games?
Sign: YOU LIKE PLAY COMPUTER GAME

Having Fun with Hobbies

Having hobbies keeps you occupied and entertained and most can be shared with Deaf friends.

Table 11-5 shows you the signs you need to know.

Table 11-5		Hobbies	
English	**Sign**	**English**	**Sign**
HOBBY/ INTEREST		SHOPPING	
GARDENING		COOKING	
RUNNING		KEEPING FIT	

English	Sign	English	Sign
DRESSMAKING		KNITTING	
READING		SEWING	

If your hobby was stamp collecting, for example, you sign, **stamp** then **collect.** The sign for **collect** is like gathering something into the palm of your hand.

English: I like collecting old books.
Sign: ME LIKE COLLECT OLD BOOKS

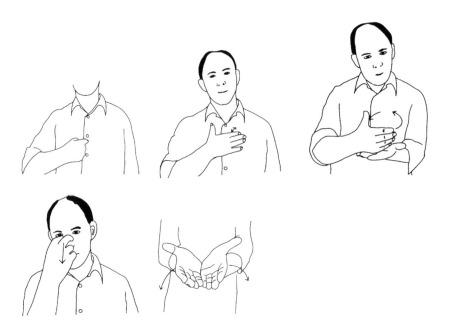

Starting to Sign

 Jean and Olga discuss their hobbies.

Jean: What are your hobbies?
Sign: YOUR HOBBIES?

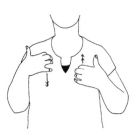

Olga: I love gardening, cooking, and reading. What are
              yours?
Sign: LOVE GARDEN, COOK, READ. YOURS?

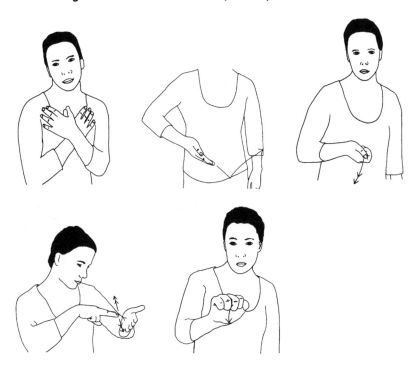

Jean: I like running and keeping fit.
Sign: ME LIKE RUN KEEP FIT

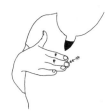

Olga: Not me! I love shopping! You like sewing?
Sign: (head shake) ME LOVE SHOPPING. YOU LIKE SEWING?

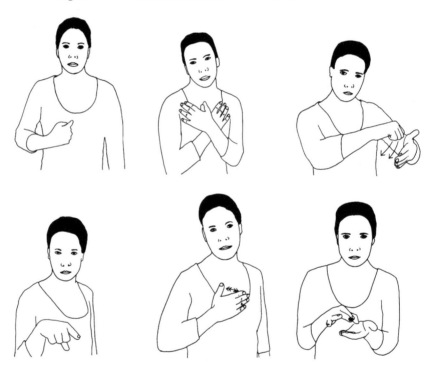

Jean: Yes, I like knitting and making my own clothes
Sign: (head nod) ME LIKE KNIT MAKE CLOTHES

 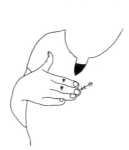 

 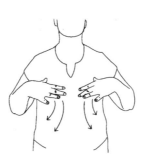

Fun & Games

Look at these signs and see whether you can remember what they are.

1.

2.

3.

4.

5.

6.

7.

8.

9.

10.

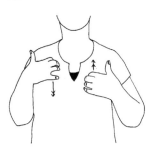

Part IV
Looking into Deaf Life

The 5th Wave   By Rich Tennant

"I've been dating a deaf girl for over 3 years. She says I communicate pretty well for a hearing person."

In this part . . .

This Part explains something of the richness and diversity of Deaf life and culture, and helps you to understand the lives Deaf people lead. Here we talk a little about the history of BSL, the hearing professionals who work with Deaf people, and some of the technological innovations that can help Deaf people come to terms with the world.

Chapter 12

Deaf Community and Culture

- -

- -

*Y*ou may have got this book in order to pick up a few signs and to be able to communicate with Deaf friends, neighbours, work colleagues or members of your family. The cultural aspects to the language may not have occurred to you. This chapter gives you a brief history of BSL, Deaf education and the social side of the Deaf community.

British Sign Language is usually referred to in its abbreviated form of BSL. The same applies to the Sign Languages of other countries, for example, ASL for American Sign Language, AUSLAN for Australian Sign Language and LSF (Langue des Signes Française) for French Sign Language.

Digging Into the History of BSL

Throughout history, sign language has been regarded as inferior and not recognised as a proper language at all, but as a system of mime and gestures. Over the centuries many references have been made to the use of signs in communicating with Deaf people.

In 1666 Samuel Pepys wrote in his diary that he observed a Deaf boy communicating with his master, giving him a report of the progress of the Great Fire of London. Following the Milan Conference on Deaf education in 1880, sign language was banned in schools for the Deaf. In those days, almost all schools for the Deaf were residential and the fact that sign language survived is thanks to certain children – who had Deaf parents who signed – using it to communicate with fellow pupils when their teachers were not watching, often in the dormitories when they were supposed to be asleep. Because the schools were all over the country and the signs were developed by the children in a natural way, then passed on to successive generations, many regional variations of BSL exist, just as accents and dialects in the hearing world. Deaf clubs also played an important part in keeping sign language alive.

Although sign language had been around for over a hundred years, it was not until 1974 that it was acknowledged that sign language is a language in its own right and officially named 'British Sign Language'. Researchers investigated the linguistics of BSL at various universities and the findings confirmed that BSL has its own formal grammatical structure and syntax.

BSL does use many English words but, because it has its own grammatical rules – based on the visual use of the hands and space – it does not use the same word order.

In 2003, the British government gave BSL official recognition as a language in its own right, but it has yet to gain the same legal status, as other traditional minority languages used in the UK, such as Welsh and Gaelic.

'D/deaf' is the term used to include those with an acquired hearing loss, or who do not use sign language (deaf) and those who are part of the Deaf community and use BSL as their first or preferred language (Deaf).

Exploring the Origins of Deaf Education

In 1760 Thomas Braidwood opened the first school for the Deaf in Edinburgh, employing a *combined method* of teaching. This used fingerspelling, sign, speech, reading, and writing. Not much was known about his methods because he was highly secretive. Only wealthy people could afford to send their children to his school. Twenty-three years later he established the Braidwood Academy for the Deaf and Dumb in Hackney, London.

In the late eighteenth and nineteenth centuries residential schools for the Deaf, such as the Royal Schools for the Deaf at Margate, Exeter, Birmingham and Manchester, were established and they all used sign language for communication.

Deaf 1880 Milan conference

In 1880 a conference of educators of the Deaf took place in Milan, Italy. The majority of the 'educators of the Deaf' present voted in favour of banning sign language in schools for the Deaf and using only oral methods of communication. This was to apply to all schools for the Deaf in Europe and the USA. Five Americans representing 6,000 Deaf pupils in the USA were the only ones who voted against it. No Deaf people were present to give their views, because Deaf people had been banned from attending.

This conference had a huge impact on sign language as Deaf teachers in Deaf schools lost their jobs and were replaced by teachers who were trained to run their classrooms using only the oral method. Signing and gestures were strictly forbidden. Deaf children were not taught or allowed to use sign language for nearly 100 years and generations of Deaf children were taught in a way that was unnatural and frustrating. Teachers harshly punished children who signed or used gestures by tying their hands to their chairs or behind their backs. They also used caning of hands.

The oral method

Teachers of the Deaf had to use this method, which relied on any residual hearing a child had (there were, of course, no hearing aids at that time), lipreading and whatever speech the child may possess.

Needless to say this method of teaching denied Deaf children any worthwhile education and many left school at the age of 16 with a reading age of 8½ years.

Enlightenment at last!

When sign language was recognised as a language in its own right in 1974, it was re-introduced into some schools that had previously used the oral method – although it was now known as Total Communication – which consisted of signing, accompanied by lipreading and speech.

It was not until the 1990s that bi-lingual education – acquiring knowledge through BSL and English – started.

The Social Side of the Deaf World

As only 10 per cent of people have Deaf parents, most Deaf people grow up in a world where their family and work colleagues are not Deaf. Communication is, more often than not, frustrating or non-existent and Deaf people often feel left out and isolated in a hearing world. Traditionally, Deaf clubs are sometimes the only places where they do not feel isolated and can participate fully in all activities.

Discovering Deaf clubs

Deaf clubs are local clubs for Deaf people where they can relax and catch up with news that is relevant to them and their friends. Committees usually run these clubs, usually consisting of a chair, secretary, treasurer, catering manager and several committee members. A typical Deaf club has activities such as indoor games, table tennis, badminton, a drama club, and social events such as whist drives, bingo, and dances (yes, Deaf people DO dance as, although they do not hear the music they usually have a good sense of rhythm). Some Deaf clubs have bars where Deaf members can buy drinks instead of having to go out to a pub. Outdoor activities include football, cricket, tennis, and bowls clubs.

Embracing the new

Though Deaf clubs play an important role in Deaf culture, modern technological developments have led to the availability of many alternative activities in which Deaf people can participate fully. These include:

- ✔ Captioned movies
- ✔ Discos
- ✔ Guided and interpreted tours of museums, art galleries, and other places of interest
- ✔ Sign language-interpreted or captioned stage performances.

Modern technology allows the younger generation of Deaf people to fax, text, or email each other easily and arrange to meet. As a result, they're not so interested in attending Deaf clubs and, as a consequence, many Deaf clubs have closed down. The young Deaf generation now prefer to meet at pubs, discos or their homes rather than have the responsibility of organising club activities. Many of them are willing to drive hundreds of miles to specially arranged events where they can meet up and socialise.

Just because people are Deaf, it does not mean they have empty lives. Deaf people may not experience everything in life the same way as those who can hear (music obviously being one of the main things they cannot take part in) but they can take part in and enjoy most of the same things that hearing people do.

Access for Deaf people – Language Service Professionals (LSPs)

It's great, and to be encouraged, for hearing people to discover the basics of BSL to help in communicating with Deaf people. But sometimes, communicating with people who just know the basics is not enough, and Deaf people have the right to access information in the same way as anyone else.

The Disability Discrimination Act (DDA) states that service providers need to make 'reasonable adjustments' to ensure access for Deaf people. As communication is a basic need for all humans, occasions therefore occur when getting in the professionals is the most appropriate adjustment to ensure that Deaf people have the right access to the services and information they require. So who are the professionals and what, exactly, do they do?

Investigating interpreters

Most people's exposure to sign language interpreters is through seeing an animated man or woman popping up in the corner of their TV screen on certain programmes like *Hollyoaks* on a Sunday, or on the news. This man or woman is interpreting into BSL everything that is being said on the programme, so that Deaf people have access in their own language. You may ask: 'Why can't Deaf people just read the subtitles instead?' The answer is, many can. But many Deaf people don't use English as their first language – they use BSL. People writing the subtitles use written English, whereas interpreters sign in BSL.

Interpreters can be used everywhere and anywhere. In fact, wherever a Deaf BSL user needs access in their own language! You can book an interpreter through an agency, or as a freelance worker. They can be booked by the Deaf person themselves, or by a hearing person – maybe an employer, or a theatre manager, doctor, or office administrator. As so few fully qualified, registered BSL interpreters exist for the 70,000 Deaf people who use BSL (approximately 500 qualified interpreters have registered at present in the UK), you need to book an interpreter with as much advance notice as possible. Due to the shortage, many Deaf people rely on registered trainee interpreters (TIs), still undergoing interpreter training, or even junior trainee interpreters (JTIs), still studying for their sign language qualifications. All registered interpreters abide by a code of ethics and practice, to ensure that they're providing an adequate standard of service at an appropriate level for the client.

An interpreter interprets everything that is said, in the way that the individual says it. Speech is much more than just the words being spoken . . . much of the information given is in the *way* that people speak the words – the tone of voice, intonation, the volume, and pitch. And the Deaf person needs to have access to that too! An interpreter, then, has to convey not only the content of the message, but the way in which that message is delivered. So if you're speaking sloppily or almost falling over with informality, the interpreter matches that in BSL. You may both end up on the floor!

The interpreter listens to the message in English, processes it, then produces it in BSL. As this is all happening simultaneously, there is a slight time delay. If you're being interpreted, you don't need to wait for the interpreter to catch up with you – so don't separate your words out. The interpreter is often waiting for you to finish your phrase or sentence so the interpretation of the language into BSL can happen. So just let the interpreter do what they need to do. If they can't hear you properly, or you're talking like Speedy Gonzalez, they will take appropriate measures.

Of course, an interpreter doesn't just translate from English into BSL. Much of an interpreter's job involves interpreting the other way too . . . that is, from BSL into spoken English. Deaf people do not exist just to be spoken at – they have something to say! An interpreter is trained in understanding BSL and ensuring that BSL is correctly translated into spoken language – with all that spoken English entails (tone of voice, intonation, vocabulary, and so on). This is commonly known as 'voice-over'. So if a Deaf person is signing formally, an interpreter puts that into formal speech and matches the formal BSL signs to the equivalent words in English. And if a Deaf person wants to swear in BSL, an interpreter interprets that into the appropriate swear word in English. That's access for you. So don't get upset at the interpreters – they're just doing their job!

Formal, informal, and colloquial are all types of *register*. An interpreter is trained to match the register of whoever is speaking or signing, when interpreting into the other language.

If you're using a BSL/English interpreter to talk to a Deaf person, make sure that the Deaf person is able to see both you and the interpreter. The information is coming from you, and you use mannerisms, body language and facial expressions that the Deaf person wants to see. The interpreter and the speaker need to be standing as near to each other as possible. The interpreter doesn't necessarily need to see the speaker all the time, but does need to hear what's being said.

Communicators/Communication Support Workers (CSWs)

Communicators have not undergone interpreter training or reached the same level in BSL as an interpreter. However, they're highly skilled professionals who use a variety of communication strategies to meet the access needs of a Deaf, deafened, or hard of hearing person. Communicators, or Communication Support Workers (CSWs), may use a combination of sign language and note taking or clear speech supported by signs or gestures – whatever is the chosen method of the Deaf person. Education typically uses communicators, such as in schools and colleges where a Deaf student has a variety of support needs. The CSW may be responsible for modifying the English in exam questions or handouts, and annotating paperwork to provide better access. Sometimes CSWs are trained to support deaf blind people, using the deaf-blind manual alphabet to make words into the deaf blind person's palm.

More communicators than qualified interpreters work in the UK, and sometimes a Deaf person chooses to use a communicator they know and feel comfortable with, rather than a fully qualified interpreter – that's their prerogative! However, unlike the situation with interpreters, because no national, independent register of CSWs exists, therefore, there is no national benchmark to ensure quality standards either. As such, many communicators are employed by organisations who have their own internal codes of practice and ethics, which the CSW would come under.

Lipspeakers

Let's say you fall into the category of a deaf person who doesn't know BSL. Maybe you've acquired your hearing loss later in life, or maybe you've been deaf from birth but just been brought up using the oral method (see the section 'The oral method' above). It may be that you're used to lipreading as your main method of communicating, and feel quite comfortable with lipreading on a daily basis. On a one-to-one level with people you know, and whose lip patterns you're familiar with, this is not causing you many difficulties. However, make a trip to the doctor who has that strange accent or try a conversation with the man in the post office who sports a big handle-bar moustache, and you're struggling. A training course or a meeting at work is a nightmare – everyone is talking at different speeds. You can't keep up, you don't know most of them and they're too far away to lipread anyway. Time to bring in 'the professionals'!

CULTURAL WISDOM

Mixing methods of communication

If the deaf client knows how to fingerspell, the lipspeaker may use fingerspelling to indicate the first letter of a word that is hard to lipread. For example the sound 'G' as in 'girl' or 'C' as in 'cool' can't be seen on the lips, so the letter is shown by fingerspelling, if 'G' or 'C' is the first letter of the word. Also, a lipspeaker will spell the first letters of any names. Numbers can also be shown on the hands – 18 and 80 look nearly identical on the lips!

A lipspeaker is someone who is trained to use their speech patterns effectively for lipreaders in relaying information from another source. Instead of the deaf person having to lipread the man with the moustache, the lady with the strong accent, the group of chatty people, the lipreader lipreads from just one person – the lipspeaker. A lipspeaker has been trained to speak clearly in a way that is more lipreadable, but without using their voice. As you can imagine, it would be a little distracting for everyone else if there was a constant echo after anything was said. Instead, a lipspeaker sits or stands opposite the lipreader, and silently repeats everything that is being said. The lipspeaker would indicate who is speaking by a slight gesture of the hand, and would ensure that they're a few words behind what is being said. Why is this necessary? Well, some people speak fast, others speak slowly and hesitate, mumble their words, and add lots of 'umms and aahs'. . .all these things affect what is happening on the lips, and make lipreading really hard work. By staying a few words behind (and exercising a good deal of short-term memory!) the lipspeaker can repeat what is being said, but at a more lipreadable pace. A bit of time also allows the lipspeaker to get rid of those 'redundant' words like 'umm' and 'aah' so that the lipreader can make more sense of what's being said.

But what about all the tone of voice, the intonation, the way people say the words? How does the lipreader have access to that? The lipspeaker, being a highly trained and skilled sort, uses appropriate facial expressions and gestures to communicate the manner in which someone is speaking. A blank face makes lipreading much more difficult, and a lipspeaker with a constantly expressionless countenance would put the lipreader to sleep quickly. So to give the same access that hearing people get – the lipspeaker shows this on her face and in her eyes. Of course, if the speaker is pretty boring and monotonous, the lipspeaker has the challenge of having to convey that too . . . hoping that her client is not thinking that she is the one who is boring!

Manual notetakers

Take a Deaf student attending a university lecture, for example. She is watching the sign language interpreter at the front, so would struggle to take adequate notes at the same time. So that a Deaf person has the same access as their hearing peers, a note-taker may be provided. The note taker would keep a written record of as much as possible that is being said, using precis, symbols and abbreviations as appropriate. This means that the Deaf student has a set of notes, on paper, to take away with her at the end of the lecture/seminar/meeting.

Other deaf students who don't use BSL interpreters may choose to use a note taker as their principle means of support. In this case, the note taker would normally sit beside the deaf person, so that the notes can be read over their shoulder, giving the deaf person access to what's going on. The note taker, in this situation, would aim to take down as much as possible – not only the topic information, but any asides, comments, jokes, announcements . . . even the moans and complaints of their fellow students. Watch for the smoke rising from the note taker's fingers!

Electronic note-takers

Electronic note takers do what it says on the tin. They take notes electronically! Sometimes the note taker's laptop is connected to another laptop which the Deaf person uses. The note taker taps out the notes, and they come up on both screens. Other note takers just use one laptop, and save the notes in an electronic file, which can then be put on a disc or memory stick for the Deaf person, or sent as an attachment via email. The advantage of electronic note taking is that it can be quicker (depending on your typing speed!) and mistakes can neatly be deleted rather than manually erased as with paper and pen. It also avoids the problem of spidery handwriting . . . a real barrier to anyone!

Electronic note takers can also be useful in workshops, lectures, meetings and training events where more than one deaf person is in attendance. The laptop is connected to a projector, which can project the notes onto a big screen so that anyone can read them. Those who do not sign and do not lipread, but want access to what's going on, in written English, can make particular use of electronic note takers.

A Deaf person who uses a note taker needs to be able to read and understand English grammar, as the notes would be taken in written English . . . if you're in England, that is!

Palantypist/speech-to-text reporter (STTR)

A palantypist (or STTR) uses a special 'phonetic' keyboard (different to the normal QWERTY keyboard that electronic note takers use. The keyboard is attached to a computer, which changes the phonetic input into English words, and projects them for all to see onto a large screen or TV. The benefit of palantype is that it can be really fast, and can ensure a verbatim record of what is being said that is also instantaneous. This means that Deaf or hard of hearing people can keep right on track and don't have to rely on lipreading . . . especially when the speaker decides to turn the lights off for a slide show (even the best lipreaders can't lipread in the dark!).

LSP etiquette

LSPs – like any professionals – provide a service, and have most likely undergone years of training to achieve their qualifications so they can offer a high standard of service. Language service professionals should follow a code of professional conduct and ethics. The code of ethics needs to include things such as confidentiality and impartiality. Most LSPs are members of a register and sign up to the national professional code of practice. This code has real benefits, as it provides assurance for the client that she is getting someone who is suitably qualified and abides by working guidelines. It also provides an avenue for complaints, if that becomes necessary!

Because of the national shortage of all language service professionals for Deaf people, they're busy bees, and you may need to book one well in advance. They need to know as much information about the booking as possible. Bear these points in mind:

- ✔ Where should they sit/stand?
- ✔ What's the name of the contact person?
- ✔ What's the name of the Deaf client?
- ✔ How long is the booking?
- ✔ Will there be breaks?

Sometimes it is necessary for LSPs to co-work (for example, two interpreters working together). Co-working BSL interpreters, for example, often swap over every 20 minutes or so depending on the length and density of the assignment. Interpreting can be physically and mentally exhausting, so two co-workers can ensure a higher quality of service. We're talking about human beings after all – not machines!

LSPs also need to know what the assignment's about. They may want to know whether the assignment includes:

- ✔ Specific terminology or jargon?
- ✔ Extensive use of acronyms?
- ✔ Video clips
- ✔ Microsoft Windows® PowerPoint presentations
- ✔ Songs or poetry?

Giving 'the professionals' as much prior information as possible means they can do a much better job . . . which makes everyone happy!

If LSPs feel unable to take on a booking – they will let you know. It may be that they don't feel comfortable with the subject matter, or don't feel suitably qualified or experienced to do that particular assignment. One interpreter may have lots of experience interpreting in court/legal settings, but feel out of his depth interpreting at a Catholic priestly ordination ceremony, or vice versa. That's why letting them know what the assignment involves helps to ensure that the interpreter doesn't bite off more than he can chew.

Language service professionals need breaks! Break times mean switch-off time and a trip to the loo . . . so don't ask them to work at such times, no matter how informal your 'chat' with the Deaf person may be. And don't feel you have to make small talk and tell them all about your best friend's cousin's sister's great grandma who wore hearing aids once . . . however fascinating it may be.

Chapter 13

Technology and Modifications for Deaf People

In This Chapter

▶ Introducing various technical devices used by Deaf people

▶ Understanding how the technology works

▶ Knowing what to do – and what not to

*I*n this chapter, we talk about the ways Deaf people stay in touch through the use of technology. We look at how to make effective use of the phone line and how to use other bits and pieces to communicate.

Throughout the chapter we refer to Deaf (with a capital 'D') people, that is, BSL users who are members of the Deaf community. However, much of the technology we talk about is used be other deaf (small 'd') people, who don't sign.

Keeping in Touch

Let's say it loud and clear: A Deaf person is never going to be sitting by the phone, waiting for it to ring. Unless you've enough hearing to make sense of speech, you're not going to be able to chat away on a standard telephone. And a Deaf person who appears to cope quite well when you talk to them face-to-face may not be able to communicate with you in the same way down the phone. One reason for this difference is that speech sounds different down a telephone to when you're in the same room. Even if you have a little bit of hearing (residual hearing), which many Deaf people may have if they're using hearing aids, it's quite a different ball game when channelled down a phone line – whether you're going through a tunnel on a train, or not. Another reason is that you can't see the person you're talking to. This fact is pretty important for a Deaf person who likes to see your facial expressions and lip patterns.

Don't ask to speak to a Deaf person on the phone, unless you're absolutely sure that they can use the phone and whatever you do, don't bellow down it. It won't help, and you may not get the response you were hoping for!

Do not make a call on behalf of a Deaf person, then pass them the handset. You're making that call for them because they can't use the phone!

So, without the phone, how *do* Deaf people keep in touch?

Minicoms and Text-phones

No public service organisation should be without one of these phones, and they now come in all shapes and sizes. Some are portable, some sit permanently on a desk next to, or in place of, a telephone. A text-phone is a popular piece of equipment used by Deaf people to communicate through the telephone, as it involves typing and reading rather than relying on speaking, or listening to speech. People with speech impairments, therefore, also use text-phones. Text-phones (also commonly known as minicoms) make use of a normal phone line. Some may have the phone line permanently connected, meaning that you make the call directly from the machine, and others may contain two circular pads, on which the standard telephone is placed after the call is made and connected.

Once two people are connected using text-phones, they can hold a live conversation by typing messages to each other. Text-phoning is not really like internet messenger services, where you have to wait a few minutes while your friend painstakingly taps out a sentence and presses 'return'. Instead, with a minicom, you can see every letter the other person types, as they type it. And their spelling errors too! So if you make a mistake, then delete it, the other person sees you deleting those letters from their end. No hiding it! To avoid overlapping and interrupting each other throughout the typed conversation, a few 'minicom manners' have developed to help things run smoothly. For example, if you get to the end of your sentence and want the other person to respond, you can type 'GA' meaning 'Go Ahead'. At the end of the conversation, each person types 'SK' (Stop Keying) to say goodbye and signify the end. This code is much more polite than just hanging up!

About text-phone 'language'. . . if a Deaf person is a BSL user, it may mean that BSL is their first language, and English their second (or even third or fourth) language. As BSL is not a written language, the user may not be familiar with English written grammar. You may notice that questions, for example, may be written in a different way to standard English grammar, and show a more BSL way of structuring a sentence. An example may be 'you work where?' or 'your name what?'. So if you find it difficult to read what someone is typing on the text-phone, it may just be a language issue. Or it may of course also be that the minicom is not working properly or the connection's been lost (as can easily happen!)

Type-Talk and Text-Direct

Can you call a Deaf person, who has a minicom, if you don't have one yourself? Yes you can! You can with the help of a useful relay service called 'Text-Direct', which is operated by RNID TypeTalk. Using a normal phone, a hearing person can dial a prefix number (18002), then the Deaf person's full telephone number, and automatically a TypeTalk operator comes into the call, and everything you say is relayed by the operator who types your message to the Deaf person, who reads it on their text-phone. Likewise, when the Deaf person types a message back, the operator reads out exactly what is typed to the hearing person on the other end of the line. In the same way, using this service, a Deaf person can have access to anyone who has a telephone (for example, friends, doctors, businesses) by using their minicom. The prefix number for the text-phone user is 18001, then the full telephone number of the other person. As you can imagine, this service is highly useful, meaning that a Deaf person has instant access, by means of their own text-phone.

If a Deaf person wants to contact the emergency services (999), they can dial 18000 from their text-phone. All information is then relayed via text-phones.

SMS

These days, nobody seems to be without a mobile phone. And Deaf people are no exception. Using SMS, Deaf people can stay in touch and have 'text-chats' in the same way that anyone can. Some of the great things about texting are the speed, the directness, that you don't need any specialist technology (even most landline phones have an SMS function), you don't need a third person to relay a message, and you don't need a great grasp of written English! Text messages tend to be short, to the point, and contain their own spelling peculiarities that cross the Deaf/hearing cultural divide. 'Want go2 def club 2nite? c u L8r. ;o)'

Fax machines

Some may say that fax machines have had their day, because everyone's using email. But a fax machine is a useful piece of equipment to have, at home or in the office. What can you do with faxes that you can't so easily do in emails? Draw diagrams and pictures! You can also annotate things, circle bits of information, scribble things out, modify language in a way that you may not so easily be able to do with emails, unless you're a technical whiz.

Such differences make fax machines a useful piece of technology for Deaf people who predominantly use BSL to communicate. Deaf people find emails useful too, of course, but writing emails requires a fair amount of knowledge of written English, which may be a barrier to some. So you can be more visual and creative with your pen, if you have access to a fax machine.

Email

Of course, Deaf people use email too! And now with every office in every organisation dependent on email, this technology has made an enormous difference to Deaf people in employment in positions that may until recently have required speaking, listening, and using a telephone. Email keeps everyone in contact on an equal level – hearing or Deaf, whether among colleagues, friends, or for business.

Videophones/webcams

Using videophones and webcams in communication has great potential – especially among Sign Language users. Unlike with email, text-phones, and SMS, you don't need any knowledge of the English language to use a webcam or videophone, and this aspect of the technology is great if you prefer to use BSL instead. Evidently, this technology is likely to be of huge benefit for Deaf Sign Language users who want to be able to contact friends using their first language. The technology at the moment is a little expensive and the picture quality needs to be pretty top-notch to make good use of it for sign language, but things are improving all the time. So who knows? Videophones may be commonplace and as cheap as mobiles in the years to come. Watch this space!

Wakey-wakey! Flashing Lights and Vibrating Alarms

Modern technology provides a whole bunch of useful gadgets to enable Deaf people to know when something or someone needs their attention. Or simply that they need to get up in the morning.

Somebody at the door

You have no excuse for avoiding that double-glazing salesman at your door, thanks to modern technology. A variety of devices can be installed to inform a Deaf person that somebody is at the door. They range from wiring up the doorbell so that the ceiling lights flash if it's rung (a bit like having a disco in your own home), to more complex technology that sends signals to a portable unit or pager that flashes or vibrates to tell you that someone is waiting patiently outside. Of course, one benefit of this technology may be that the salesman thinks the doorbell is broken as he can't hear it ringing, or see the flashing lights inside, and moves on to your neighbour instead.

Fire! Fire!/Baby's crying!

A crying baby may not give his parents much peace, and Deaf people can't escape the crying any more than the rest of us. Thanks to popular technical devices like pager systems, Deaf people can be alerted to the baby crying, or fire alarms, smoke detectors, and phones. These devices mean that wherever you are in the house, you can be alerted by the pager through a variety of identifiable signals: For example different lights may be displayed or different vibrations felt, which correspond to a particular alert. Just be careful not to get the alerts confused and drench the baby with a fire extinguisher!

Wake-up call

Unless you sleep under the stars and the sun wakes you up in the morning, you're likely going to need a little help to bring you into the land of the living. Some alarm clocks are modified to include flashing lights, or the bedside lamp can be set to turn on at wake-up time. Other Deaf people may prefer a vibrating alarm that goes under the pillow and shake-wakes them up, or a vibrating wrist-watch can be worn at night How one person prefers to wake up is obviously up to individual preference. And technology is just one option among many possibilities, including man, woman or beast!

Part V
The Part of Tens

The 5th Wave   By Rich Tennant

In this part . . .

This is a *For Dummies* book, so there must be a Part of Tens. The five chapters in this part offer a range of fascinating tips and insights on how to become a better signer, and how to understand Deaf culture more fully.

Here we also provide you with ten phrases to remember if you forget everything else, and some tip top resources to help you broaden your knowledge of Deaf culture in general, and BSL in particular.

Chapter 14

Ten Top Tips To Improve Your Signing Skills

....

In This Chapter

▶ Helping communication along

▶ Showing emotion

▶ Keeping it honest

▶ Discovering practice methods

....

*T*his chapter gives you ten top tips to make you a more proficient BSL signer. Follow the advice here to polish up your basic skills.

Watch My Face

Deaf people feel uncomfortable if you just focus on their hands when they sign to you. A lot of important information is obtained from facial expressions and lipreading, so look at the signer's face and lips; you can still see their hands in your peripheral vision.

RSVP Please

Have you ever talked to a person and been disconcerted by their lack of response? Deaf people are particularly sensitive to such a lack of response so, when they sign to you, do show that you understand what they say by smiling or nodding your head in appropriate places, raising an eyebrow or making little signing comments such as 'really?' or 'I don't believe it'. These comments encourage the signer and help the conversation along.

Showing the Sign!

Remember to show your emotions when you sign. Deaf people are naturally expressive and you may find it hard at first to be the same as you have probably been brought up to 'not pull faces'. Expressiveness is an important part of BSL. Think of the actors in the old silent movies having to show everything in their faces because there was no spoken dialogue – think 'Charlie Chaplin' when you sign.

Spotting the Difference

Just as hearing people have different ways of talking, Deaf people have different ways of signing. People speak slowly or fast, some use monosyllables, some 'go round the houses', some make themselves clear and some are difficult to understand. You may meet just as wide a variety of signing styles so don't think 'seen one, seen them all'.

Being Honest

One of the worst things you can do when talking to a signer is to pretend that you understand when she can tell perfectly well that you don't. If you don't understand something, don't be afraid to ask for a repetition. Deaf people would much rather repeat something two or more times than carry on talking when they know that you do not understand. Show that you're trying and they will be patient and helpful. Don't be in too much of a hurry to interrupt and ask for a repetition though, trying to pick out a few signs and the context they are used in may give you a good idea of what the person is saying and enable you to give an appropriate response.

Mirror, Mirror, on the Wall

Some people recommend that you practise your signing in front of a mirror and though using a mirror enables you to see what you look like when you sign to someone, you may not find it that useful. If you do want to see what you look like to other people, use a mirror mainly to see what your signing space is like – is your signing too big or – more likely – small. You can also check whether your expressions accurately convey the meaning of the signs.

Being a Film Star

If you have a camcorder, use it to film yourself signing. Then watch it back afterwards to get a more accurate idea of your signing skills than you would by watching yourself in a mirror. Try to find a fellow signing novice to share the film session with you as signing to somebody else is more natural than signing to the camera and you can give each other feedback afterwards when watching the playback. You can also ask for feedback from your tutor, if you have one.

Keeping a Record

If you do use a camcorder, a good method of checking your progress is to sign a favourite poem or song at intervals of a few weeks – with practice in between – over a period of time you should become much more fluent.

Hare or Tortoise?

Practise your finger-spelling as much as you can, preferably with a fellow signing beginner. If you can become adept at finger-spelling, you always have a method of communicating with a Deaf person. It is obviously slower to spell out everything rather than sign but you WILL get there at the end. A good way to practise and become more fluent is to spell out Mary Poppins' famous 'supercalifragilisticexpialidocious' – try timing yourself and see how fast you can bring your time down – but no cheating! For more on finger-spelling refer to Chapter 2.

The Way of the World

The best way to absorb a foreign language is to go and live in the country where is the language is spoken. If you read books about deafness or infor-mation leaflets from organisations for and of the Deaf, you gain an under-standing of the Deaf World, or Deaf Culture (as some people call it). This information often gives you clues as to what a Deaf person is talking about. For more on Deaf community and culture see Chapter 12.

Chapter 15

Ten Top Tips For Good Communication

*I*n this chapter, we look at ten top tips for good communication with Deaf people. By keeping in mind things like your body language, positioning, and being clear in your speech, communication can change from being a frustrating experience, to being an enriching challenge that encourages both parties – Deaf and hearing. The most important thing to remember about communication is: be flexible and don't give up. Read on for more pointers.

Get an Attitude

Communicating with any deaf person – whether they're BSL users or not – is all about having the right attitude. If you really want to understand, and be understood, you're already half-way there. BSL is not mime, not just body language, and not an inferior form of English. BSL is a full, rich, living language in its own right that has its own structures and grammar, changing vocabulary, weird and wonderful expressions, jargon, slang, swear words, and technical terms. And the Deaf people who use it vary in their ability to use BSL, as hearing people vary in their ability to use English. The right attitude to have towards BSL is to appreciate its wealth, its worth, and its community.

Take no notice of what you've been told or read in the newspaper. A monkey may be able to pick up a few signs, but that doesn't make it a BSL user, no more than a talking parrot is a fluent speaker of English!

Lights, Camera . . . Action!

Before you even open your mouth, or lift your hands to start signing, make sure that you've got the Deaf person's attention. To do this you need to get eye contact, and this can be done in a number of ways, according to the situation and the person. Refer to Chapter 1 for 'getting attention' ideas other than waving your hands. Once you've established eye contact, consider what you want to say and how to say it. Have a piece of paper and pen nearby in case you need to write things down. If you're communicating with someone who doesn't use a lot of English, don't be too heavy on the complex words yourself. Get to the point, try not to mumble, and remember to keep your face visible. Loosen up your body and add gestures! And let your whole face – not just your lips, do the talking.

Does He Take Sugar?

Deaf people are deaf not dead. And they're not dumb (in the sense of stupid). You don't need to go through someone else to ask them a question. Ask them yourself! If you're not sure whether the Deaf person understands you – give it a go anyway. Deaf people are used to having to work at communication with hearing people, and will let you know if you need to say it again, or write something down. You'd find it pretty annoying to be left out of a conversation or treated like you're invisible, wouldn't you? So give them the opportunity to decline your kind offer of a cuppa themselves. If you're using a BSL interpreter, you still need to address the Deaf person directly. After all, it's not the interpreter you're talking to, they're just there to provide communication access. The interpreter interprets everything you say, in the way you say it – so no off-the-cuff remarks 'just for the interpreter'. If the interpreter hears it, they sign it. That's equal access! For more on interpreters, refer to Chapter 12.

Get Body-Conscious

Have you ever been told that your body is your finest asset? Well, believe it when you want to communicate with Deaf people. A Deaf sign language user is expert at reading the information coming from your body . . . so beware! Use this knowledge to your advantage in communication, and make use of the common everyday gestures that we all know. Use a thumbs-up sign when talking about something good or positive. Use thumbs down for negative. Use pointing to refer to things, use your fingers to show walking, open your hands and shrug your shoulders to say you don't know. Sign language is a gestural language, so if you get used to using common gestures when speaking to a Deaf person, it'll help when picking up certain BSL signs.

When you use gestures – still keep using lip patterns as well. Unless you're using Sign Language properly, the gesture on its own may be ambiguous as you're using it in isolation, without any language to support it. If you're not confident enough to use BSL, keep using the English language, and add gestures too.

What's the Point?

We all know people who are expert in the art of waffling. It can be hard enough listening to someone constantly rambling off the point and jumping from one topic of conversation to another. If you're Deaf, and faced with a waffler, you're not going to have an easy ride in communication. Lipreading is greatly helped by knowing the context, so make sure that you establish this context from the start, and then try to stick to your point. That way, the conversation is likely to run more smoothly because the Deaf person has more opportunity to follow what you're talking about. You really don't need to talk in coochy-coo baby language (unless you're talking to a baby perhaps), but it does help if you keep your sentences fairly concise and don't take 100 words just to ask where the nearest loo is.

Keep Clear – Access Required

'Infamy! Infamy! They've all got it in for me!' shrieked Kenneth Williams in _Carry On Cleo_. The thing is, if you're not clear about what you want to say, and how you say it, it can lead to all sorts of misunderstandings and confusion. If the person you're talking to has a puzzled look on his face, he may not have got what you're saying and be working really hard to make sense of it all. Don't worry about pausing and check with them that they've understood. Don't just rattle on, hoping they work it out in the end. Check. Then try again. Make yourself clear in your speech, and clear in your signs. If you're having a go at BSL, take your time and try to relax. If you get too nervous, your hands may start to shake and be all fingers and thumbs. Clarity is more important than speed. If you're using your voice, don't shout. Just speak more clearly (but keep it natural too! No rubber lips please!) Don't over-exaggerate, but pronounce your words properly – this precision helps with lipreading. Clarify with appropriate gestures or signs, and keep your face clear of hands, books, pens . . . and fancy-dress masks.

Be Environmentally Friendly

You don't need to be an eco-warrior to make your environment more Deaf-friendly. Just being aware of some of the barriers to good communication helps to get rid of them.

If you can, move to somewhere quieter, or reduce background noise if possible. Lipreading requires concentration so it helps if the environment is calmer and less distracting. Contrary to popular belief, Deaf people do not all live in a nice quiet world. If you wear a hearing aid, you probably pick up a lot of noise and clatter as hearing aids amplify most sounds. This is why some Deaf people prefer to turn their hearing aids off when a lot of people are around.

Deaf BSL users are visual people; they receive information through their eyes. So the visual environment is going to help or hinder good communication. Be aware of what's behind and around you when you're speaking or signing. A visually busy background with lots of posters, TV screens or people walking back and forth, can be distracting if you're trying to concentrate. Likewise, the environment needs to be light enough for the Deaf person to be able to see your face. Standing in front of a window is a big communication no-no. Shadow will obscure your face. If you see light at the end of the tunnel – come into it!

One at a Time Please!

Unlike mothers and school teachers, Deaf people don't have eyes in the back of their heads. They can only look at one pair of lips or hands at a time. So remember that when you're in a group situation, it helps if people talk one at a time. If the Deaf person is lipreading, they need to know who is speaking and when, and be given a few moments to adjust to a new face. Raising your hands to indicate who is wanting to speak, in a meeting or group discussion, helps as the Deaf person then knows who to turn towards. If a BSL interpreter is being used, he is only able to interpret one person at a time. Interpreters only have one pair of arms and interpreter training has yet to provide extra limbs.

English versus BSL

English and BSL are not same thing! BSL has its own grammar and structure and its own idioms and phrases that are unique to BSL and different to the English language. When someone is signing in BSL, they do not sign word-for-word. Some of their signs may occasionally be accompanied by English word lip patterns. However, they don't follow English grammar – they use BSL grammar and use their 'signing space' to convey time, tense, direction, and many other linguistic features. If you see someone signing at the same time as speaking, using English grammar and word order, that's not BSL – what you see is SSE (Sign Supported English) or Signed Exact English (where even word endings like *–ing* and *–ed* are fingerspelt). SSE is mostly used by deaf people who rely on lipreading and the English language and like to use signs to aid communication. Members of the Deaf community use BSL, and may know English too, but possibly as a second, or even third or fourth language, depending on what they've been brought up with.

As the grammar is so different, an SSE user and a BSL user may not be able to understand each other, even though both use signing.

Don't Give Up!

Communication breakdowns always cause problems, and can happen often. The most important thing to remember is to be flexible and don't give up. As the saying goes: 'If at first you don't succeed, try, try again'.

Never say to a Deaf person 'Oh never mind, it doesn't matter'. It does matter! Giving up communicates that you're not willing to try, and can cause confusion and hurt, and make the Deaf person feel left out and unvalued.

If you do have a communication breakdown, tactics you can use to repair the breakdown and get back on track include the following:

- ✔ If a deaf person (whether Deaf, hard of hearing or deafened) doesn't understand you, first of all, try repeating yourself; two or three times at the most – don't go on and on ad nauseum.

- ✔ If repeating it doesn't help, try rephrasing. That is, say it in a different way. For example, 'How do take your tea?' may be rephrased to 'Do you take milk and sugar?'. They may not have understood the word 'tea' but may get the words 'milk and sugar'.

- ✔ OK, so you've repeated, you've tried rephrasing – what next? Use a gesture! For 'tea', maybe make a 'T' shape with your hands, or make a simple gesture of sipping from a cup.

- ✔ Use your face! So much can be communicated through facial expressions – feelings, questions, like, dislike. Practise in the mirror and don't be embarrassed.

✔ If all that doesn't work, you can always write it down. But you probably don't need to write down the whole sentence. It may be just one or two words that haven't been understood. Just write down those two words, then carry on using clear speech and signs as appropriate.

If you don't have pen and paper on you, write the word clearly on the palm of your hand, using your finger. Don't write on their hand – unless they're deafblind! And don't use a pen!

If you're communicating with a Deaf BSL user, and you don't know the sign for something, try spelling the word out using the fingerspelling alphabet (if you can remember it).

If you're resorting to writing things down for a BSL user, try to use avoid jargon and long complex sentences. It may be that they don't know the English terms or grammar. Use familiar everyday words and shorter sentences, as appropriate.

Chapter 16

Ten Top BSL Resources

A wide range of resources exist to help you broaden your knowledge of British Sign Language. In this chapter, we list ten of the best.

Honing Your Skills at BSL Classes

The best way to discover BSL is to go to your local adult education centre or college and enrol on a BSL class at Level 1. You acquire the skills best by watching a tutor demonstrate hand and body movements, and facial expressions. Being in a class also gives you more opportunities to practise with others at the same level as yourself.

Attending a Communication Club

Many Deaf people go to their local deaf club to just let their hair down and socialise with their friends. Although they welcome novice signers at their club, try not to take too much advantage of their goodwill. Do not feel offended if they do not seem to want to enter into a lengthy conversation with you. Most of them have had to cope with communicating with hearing colleagues at work during the day and want to relax and talk to their Deaf friends in their leisure time. You may have been in a similar situation when you have tried your schoolboy/girl French on holiday abroad and had to put up with pitying smiles and uncomprehending frowns from a French person so be understanding and do not monopolise someone for too long. The club organisers know of this problem, so they often set up a Communication Club where novices can practise with volunteer Deaf people. Find out from your local Deaf club whether they have such a club and how often it meets. For more on Deaf clubs, see Chapter 12.

Going to Deaf Pubs

More and more Deaf people go to 'Deaf pubs' as they are called, but Deaf pubs are not for Deaf people only. They meet maybe once a month at a particular pub, where they know other Deaf people go, to socialise with their friends and maybe make new ones. Going to a Deaf pub can be a good way to improve your signing as you can just sit back and watch and try to understand what people are signing until you feel confident enough to try to join in. Introduce yourself to a group you may be watching first and explain that you're a beginner – so they won't think you're just being nosey. They may try to bring you into the conversation, which can help to improve your *productive* (signing to others) and *receptive* (reading others') signing skills. If you attend a BSL class, ask your teacher whether she knows of such a pub and if not, try to find one on the Internet.

Taking a Trip to the Theatre or Cinema

Many theatres now provide captions or sign language-interpreted performances. Many Deaf people attend these performances regularly, so not only can you see how the interpreter signs the dialogue, but you may also discover a great way to meet different people. Captioning is a way of converting the spoken word into text on a screen at the back of and above the stage and provides access to live performances for Deaf, deafened, and hard of hearing people. Look up www.stagetext.co.uk on the Internet to find out where captioned performances are held. Enter *BSL interpreted plays* on an Internet search engine and you get a list of where a performance is BSL interpreted. Some venues hold performances where all actors are Deaf and using BSL from time to time. Enter *BSL plays* on the search engine for a list of such plays, times and locations.

Subtitled films won't help your signing skills but you may be interested to know that cinemas in big towns and cities now provide subtitles for the latest films on a weekly or monthly basis.

Attending Deaf Workshops and Conferences

Many organisations exist of/for the Deaf. The main ones are *The Royal National Institute for the Deaf (RNID), The National Deaf Children's Society (NDCS), The British Deaf Association (BDA) and The Council for the Advancement of Communication with Deaf people (CACDP).* They hold Annual General Meetings, usually in conjunction with workshops and conferences, which cover a wide range of topics related to deafness. Some Universities that offer Deaf Studies courses also have workshops and conferences with topics mainly on sign language, linguistics, and The Deaf Community and Culture. Some organisations organise 'silent weekends' – residential weekends – usually from Friday evening to Sunday afternoon – at which no one is allowed to use their voice. Attending such an event is a good way to improve as you *have* to use sign language all the time.

Watching BSL Signed DVDs

If you cannot get regular practice on a sign language course or with Deaf people, DVDs can be the best way to practise your receptive skills. A variety of businesses make a wide range of DVDs to meet different skill levels from levels 1 to 4. Check on the Internet which DVD is suitable for your current abilities or ask your tutor or a Deaf friend whether they can recommend one. Your local library may be a good source for DVDs, available free or at a nominal charge. If you attend a BSL class, your college library may have a range of DVDs for you to borrow. The Forest Bookshop is a good source of DVDs – you can find their contact details on the Internet.

Although BSL books can be a great help in remembering signs you have already acquired, watching DVDs is better as you can see the facial expressions, hand, body, and arm movements in three-dimensional signing.

Taking in TV Programmes

BBC2 broadcasts a weekly programme 'See Hear' for Deaf viewers at 1 p.m. on Wednesdays, with a repeat the following Wednesday at 1 a.m. in the morning. The programme covers news and issues relevant to the Deaf Community and is presented by Deaf BSL users, which offers opportunities to practise your receptive skills.

Wising Up to Websites

You can find a number of websites on the Internet that include graphics or videos of fingerspelling and sign language, for example, www.BritishSignLanguage.com, www.deafsign.com, and www.Deafclub.co.uk Others you can find by searching for 'British Sign Language' on the Internet. Have a look at www.deafstation.org, which is an information resources and news service, all presented in BSL.

Weighing Up Webcams

The Deaf Community are making good use of webcams. Unlike faxes and emails, they allow you to see the person you're talking to and to use BSL. Skype and ooVoo websites are widely used by Deaf people for face-to-face visual communication. If you have Deaf friends – or someone in your sign language class who has access to a webcam – you can practise with them.

Making Deaf Friends

Have you ever thought of what it would be like to have a Deaf friend? Would you feel inhibited? Worried about what sort of things you can do together? Don't worry, Deaf people do everything hearing people do, apart from actually hearing and, in some cases, speaking, so if you can sign you can share most things with a Deaf friend. Deaf people obviously do not go to see 'The Sound of Music' umpteen times or risk pneumonia by standing in the rain to listen to Madonna or Robbie Williams at one of their concerts. They do, however, do the same jobs, watch and discuss the same TV programmes, play the same sports, enjoy the same games, take part in quizzes, spend too much on clothes and the latest electronic gadgets, go to the same places for holidays and moan about the weather just as much as hearing people. One thing to remember though, if you have Deaf friends, is that they may have customs different from those of the hearing world – remember the saying 'When in Rome do as the Romans do'. Deaf people are proud of their language and customs, so if you want to 'fit in' you need to watch and discover and not be surprised if they behave differently or do things your hearing friends would not. For more on Deaf community and culture, refer to Chapter 12.

Chapter 17

Ten Really Useful Phrases

As with a foreign language phrase book, the ten useful phrases in this chapter help to get you through everyday situations until you become more accomplished in your signing skills. If you forget everything else, just try to remember these!

How Are You?

When meeting a deaf person you can sign this phrase after saying 'Hello'.

HOW ARE YOU?

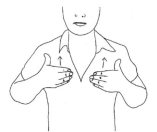 

You All Right?

You all right? can be signed in several ways. If a Deaf person greets you with this sign and a smile it means something like 'How's life?' or 'Everything OK?'. If the person says it with a concerned look, he may have heard about an illness or misfortune you've had and is enquiring if you're alright now.

ALL RIGHT?

Again, Please

If you don't understand what a deaf person is signing to you and you miss something, don't be afraid to interrupt and ask **again please**. They would rather you stop them and ask for a repeat than let them go on until they've finished and then confess you did not understand.

AGAIN   PLEASE

I'm Sorry

You may need to say **sorry** on a number of occasions. You may need to apologise for being late, arguing unnecessarily, bumping into someone, and so on, or you may need to sign it in a more heartfelt way if the person has had a loss, sad news or a misfortune. Accompany the sign by an appropriate facial expression; obviously you look more concerned if the person has had bad news. Hearing people show concern in their voices as much as their expressions but a Deaf signer needs to *show* more concern. You need to get used to showing your feelings on your face when signing.

SORRY

I Don't Understand

This phrase is often used by those new to BSL and is usually accompanied by **again please**! You need to take care when using this sign as it can mean both 'I understand' and 'I don't understand' – the meaning is changed by nodding or shaking your head as you give the sign, with a puzzled facial expression for the latter.

DON'T UNDERSTAND

Do You Need Help?

This phrase is useful if you think a deaf person needs help with something or looks lost. Be careful with the sign though: The sign going towards the other person means 'do you need help' but going towards the signer means 'I need help'. However, don't rush in with the query if you think a deaf person is in trouble communicating with a hearing person, some deaf people prefer to try a bit more themselves before asking for help.

WANT   HELP

That's Right!

The sign for **right** is the same as for the **good** sign, as shown in the Cheat Sheet Essential Expressions, but is signed with thumb sideways as shown in the illustration below. You use this phrase in various situations such as agreeing with what another person is saying, confirming that something is correct or asserting that you're right. For the latter, make the sign towards yourself.

RIGHT

That's Bad/Wrong!

The **bad** sign is the same for **wrong** – a clenched fist with little finger upright. It is used the same way as the **that's right** sign but, of course, means the opposite. It can also be used to add emphasis to an exclamation such as 'Oh dear!', 'Poor you!', 'Oh, no!', or 'What a shame!' – all with the appropriate facial expression.

BAD

Excuse Me

This phrase is often used formally or when approaching people you do not know. If you see a group of people you don't know talking and maybe blocking your way, or you want to ask them something, you sign **excuse me**. If you know the group, you would say **sorry** rather than **excuse me.**

EXCUSE

See You Around/Soon!

When taking leave of someone, you can sign **see you around,** and maybe adding **soon,** after saying goodbye, but not all Deaf people use this phrase as they and have different ways of taking leave. Find out from your friends how they say their goodbyes.

SEE

YOU

AROUND

SOON

Chapter 18

Ten Things You (Probably) Didn't Know about Deaf Culture and History

*N*ot many people are aware that sign language has been around for thousands of years and much has been written about Deaf people and their language. Socrates wrote in 422 BC, 'If we have no voice or tongue and wished to make things clear to one another, should we not try as the dumb actually do to make signs with our hands, head and person generally?' The Talmud mentions Deaf families using sign language before the birth of Jesus. This chapter is an informative way of ending this book and will, hopefully, make you want to discover more about Deaf people and their language and enrol on a Sign Language course.

British Sign Language (BSL)

BSL has been used for hundreds of years but was only recognised by the government as an official language (along with Welsh and Gaelic) in 2003 – after a prolonged campaign by the Deaf community. In common with spoken languages, BSL is different from the sign languages of other countries. The British finger-spelling alphabet uses both hands whilst the other countries use only one. For more about the development of BSL see Chapter 12.

St John of Beverley

St John of Beverly, the eighth-century Archbishop of York, was the first person to reject Aristotle's theory that the deaf were uneducatable. He taught a poor deaf boy from Hexham how to spell the letters of the alphabet and a few words and sentences. He is regarded as the first teacher of the deaf.

Early Signs of Sign Language

In 1516, Richard Carew described two deaf men in his book 'Survey of Cornwall'. He mentioned Richard Kempe and Edward Bone, two deaf men, having 'heartie laughter' and using 'passionate gestures'. Richard Carew wrote: 'Edward Bone was a servant who used mime-like signs to communicate with his Master, and a more sophisticated sign language when he met his deaf friend, Richard Kempe, who lived nearby. When they chanced to meet, would use such kind embracements, such as strange, often, and earnest tokenings . . . and other passionate gestures.'

Vows of Silence

The earliest known wedding in Britain that was conducted in a form of sign language was in 1576. A signed wedding ceremony is recorded in the parish of Leicester between Ursula Russell and Thomas Tilsye on 5 February 1576, when they took their vows in sign language.

To Read and Write – Right?

In the 1660s, Sir Christopher Wren's brother-in-law competed with another Royal Society member to see who could best encourage a deaf pupil to read and write. John Wallis and William Holder both taught deaf people by the oral method and quarrelled over claims of plagiarism. Wallis evidently changed his mind in later years when he commented that the deaf needed to be taught through signs first.

Finger-spelling Circa 1720

The finger-spelling alphabet used in BSL is closely based on a finger alphabet chart published by Daniel Defoe, author of *Robinson Crusoe* and *Moll Flanders*. In 1720, he published *The Life and Adventures of Mr Duncan Campbell,* which contains the chart of a finger-spelled alphabet – although the 'J' is missing. Only four letters are different from those used today. In 1698, an anonymous deaf person published a small booklet *Digiti Lingua,* which contained a manual alphabet chart that laid the foundation for the present finger-spelling alphabet. For more on finger-spelling, see Chapter 2.

Give Us a Bell

If it had not been for deaf people, the telephone may not have been invented? Alexander Graham Bell's experiments in trying to invent a hearing aid for his wife and mother, who were both deaf, led him to invent the telephone in 1871. He was a skilled finger-speller and taught the famous deaf/blind Helen Keller. He was connected to the Eugenics movement and had suggested that deaf people should not marry each other.

Deaf Church to Department Store

The famous Selfridges department store in Oxford Street, London was the site of the first deaf church in the UK, St Saviour's, which was built in 1873. Queen Alexandra, wife of King Edward VII, often attended the church for services. She was deaf and attended the church to enjoy the company of other deaf people and be able to follow the services – as she was an accomplished finger-speller. The church was pulled down in 1922 to make way for the department store and was rebuilt in Acton, West London, where it still stands.

The Queen Amused Others

Queen Victoria was an accomplished finger-speller and was probably the person who taught Queen Alexandra the skill. The Queen had found out how to fingerspell when she met and befriended a young deaf girl, Elizabeth

Groves and paid for her education at the London Asylum for the Deaf and Dumb. Later, when the Queen stayed at Osborne House on the Isle of Wight, she often visited a nearby post office where Elizabeth lived with her parents, after leaving her brutal husband. The Queen would spend hours communicating with Elizabeth.

Deaf to the Crowd

Lester Piggott, probably Britain's best-known jockey, never heard the crowd urging him on when he rode his huge number of winners, because he is quite deaf. His deafness was diagnosed at the age of five but he may well have been deaf from birth. Deafness certainly did not prevent him from being the race goers' favourite and winning the Derby nine times.

Part VI
Appendixes

"Conrad signs quite well, but using British Sign Language, it takes both hands and I've taught all our children never to speak with their mouths full."

In this part . . .

This book has two appendixes. Appendix A gives you all the answers to the Fun & Games sections you've encountered on your way through the book. The second tells you what you need to know about playing and using the accompanying CD.

Appendix A

Answer Key to Fun & Games

Chapter 2

1. Good luck; 2. How are you? 3. I am well.

Chapter 3

1. m; 2. k; 3. i; 4. b; 5. j; 6. n; 7. c; 8. l; 9. h; 10. f; 11. d; 12. a; 13. g; 14. e.

Chapter 4

1. c; 2. g; 3. a; 4. h; 5. f; 6. b; 7. d; 8. e.

Chapter 5

1. f; 2. b; 3. g; 4. a; 5. c; 6. e; 7. d.

Chapter 6

1. 15; 2. 48; 3. Fifth; 4. Five past ten; 5. Half past six; 6. £86; 7. £2.26; 8. How much?; 9. 32; 10. 32 years old.

Chapter 7

Answers in chapter.

Chapter 8

Answers in chapter.

Chapter 9

1. Before; 2. Tuesday; 3. Day; 4. Ramadan; 5. Month; 6. Tomorrow; 7. April;
8. Celebrate; 9. Christmas; 10. Afternoon.

Chapter 10

Answers in chapter.

Chapter 11

1. Tennis; 2. Reading; 3. Camping; 4. Chess; 5. Climbing; 6. Skating;
7. Shopping; 8. Knitting; 9. Skiing; 10. Hobby.

Appendix B

About the CD

*T*he CD which accompanies this book features a number of videos showing British Sign Language being used in real situations. It also shows you how to sign the BSL alphabet. Watch the videos in conjunction with the relevant 'Starting to Sign' section in each chapter to see how BSL is used in everyday life.

System Requirements

Make sure that your computer meets the minimum system requirements shown in the following list. If your computer doesn't match up to most of these requirements, you may have problems using the software and files on the CD. For the latest and greatest information, please refer to the ReadMe file located at the root of the CD-ROM.

✔ A PC running Microsoft Windows or Linux with kernel 2.4 or later

✔ A Macintosh running Apple OS X or later

✔ A CD-ROM drive

If you need more information on the basics, check out these books published by Wiley Publishing, Inc.: *PCs For Dummies* by Dan Gookin; *Macs For Dummies* by Edward C. Baig; *iMacs For Dummies* by Mark L. Chambers; *Windows XP For Dummies* and *Windows Vista For Dummies,* both by Andy Rathbone.

Using the CD

To install the items from the CD to your hard drive, follow these steps.

1. **Insert the CD into your computer's CD-ROM drive.**

   The license agreement appears.

   Note to Windows users: The interface won't launch if you have autorun disabled. In that case, choose Start➪Run. (For Windows Vista, choose Start➪All Programs➪Accessories➪Run.) In the dialog box that appears, type *D:\Start.exe*. (Replace *D* with the proper letter if your CD drive uses a different letter. If you don't know the letter, see how your CD drive is listed under My Computer.) Click OK.

   Note for Mac Users: When the CD icon appears on your desktop, double-click the icon to open the CD and double-click the Start icon.

   Note for Linux Users: The specifics of mounting and using CDs vary greatly between different versions of Linux. Please see the manual or help information for your specific system if you experience trouble using this CD.

2. **Read through the license agreement and then click the Accept button if you want to use the CD.**

   The CD interface appears. The interface allows you to browse the contents and install the programs with just a click of a button (or two).

What You'll Find on the CD

The following sections are arranged by category and provide a summary of the software and other goodies you'll find on the CD. If you need help with installing the items provided on the CD, refer to the installation instructions in the preceding section.

- ✔ *Shareware programs* are fully functional, free, trial versions of copyrighted programs. If you like particular programs, register with their authors for a nominal fee and receive licenses, enhanced versions, and technical support.

- ✔ *Freeware programs* are free, copyrighted games, applications, and utilities. You can copy them to as many computers as you like — for free — but they offer no technical support.

> ✔ *GNU software* is governed by its own license, which is included inside the folder of the GNU software. There are no restrictions on distribution of GNU software. See the GNU license at the root of the CD for more details.

> ✔ *Trial, demo,* or *evaluation* versions of software are usually limited either by time or functionality (such as not letting you save a project after you create it).

Dialogues

For Windows and Mac. All the examples provided in this book are located in the Author directory on the CD and work with Macintosh, Linux, Unix, and Windows 98 and later computers. These files contain much of the sample code from the book. The structure of the examples directory is

```
Author/Ch3_cities.swf
Author/Ch3_greetings.swf
Author/Ch3_whoandwhere.swf
Author/Ch4_jobs.swf
Author/Ch5_feelingmiserable.swf
Author/Ch5_heartattack.swf
Author/Ch6_johnsbirthday.swf
Author/Ch7_holidaypacking.swf
Author/Ch8_directions.swf
Author/Ch9_makingadate.swf
Author/Ch10_goingtoacafe.swf
Author/Ch10_jeansorder.swf
Author/Ch11_johnsorder.swf
Author/Ch11_olgasorder.swf
Author/Ch11_petersorder.swf
Author/Ch11_cheatsheet.swf
Author/Ch11_hobbies.swf
Author/Ch11_jameschoice.swf
Author/Ch11_jeanschoice.swf
Author/Ch11_johnschoice.swf
Author/Ch11_olgaschoice.swf
Author/Ch11_peterschoice.swf
Author/Ch11_thissummer.swf
Author/Ch11_watchingsport.swf
```

Troubleshooting

We tried our best to compile programs that work on most computers with the minimum system requirements. Alas, your computer may differ, and some programs may not work properly for some reason.

The two likeliest problems are that you don't have enough memory (RAM) for the programs you want to use, or you have other programs running that are affecting installation or running of a program. If you get an error message such as Not enough memory or Setup cannot continue, try one or more of the following suggestions and then try using the software again:

- ✓ **Turn off any antivirus software running on your computer.** Installation programs sometimes mimic virus activity and may make your computer incorrectly believe that it's being infected by a virus.

- ✓ **Close all running programs.** The more programs you have running, the less memory is available to other programs. Installation programs typically update files and programs; so if you keep other programs running, installation may not work properly.

- ✓ **Have your local computer shop add more RAM to your computer.** This is, admittedly, a drastic and somewhat expensive step. However, adding more memory can really help the speed of your computer and allow more programs to run at the same time.

Customer Care

If you have trouble with the CD-ROM, please call Wiley Product Technical Support at 800-762-2974. Outside the United States, call 317-572-3993. You can also contact Wiley Product Technical Support at http://support.wiley.com. Wiley Publishing will provide technical support only for installation and other general quality control items. For technical support on the applications themselves, consult the program's vendor or author.

To place additional orders or to request information about other Wiley products, please call 877-762-2974.

Index

• *y* •

FOR DUMMIES®

Do Anything. Just Add Dummies

UK editions

BUSINESS

Starting a Business For Dummies
978-0-470-51806-9

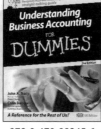

Understanding Business Accounting For Dummies
978-0-470-99245-6

Business Plans For Dummies
978-0-7645-7026-1

FINANCE

Investing For Dummies
978-0-470-99280-7

Tax For Dummies
978-0-470-99811-3

Sorting Out Your Finances For Dummies
978-0-470-69515-9

PROPERTY

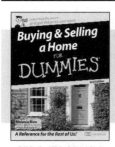

Buying & Selling a Home For Dummies
978-0-470-99448-1

Property Investing All-In-One For Dummies
978-0-470-51502-0

DIY & Home Maintenance All-In-One For Dummies
978-0-7645-7054-4

Body Language For Dummies
978-0-470-51291-3

Building Self-Confidence for Dummies
978-0-470-01669-5

Children's Health For Dummies
978-0-470-02735-6

Cognitive Behavioural Coaching For Dummies
978-0-470-71379-2

Counselling Skills For Dummies
978-0-470-51190-9

Digital Marketing For Dummies
978-0-470-05793-3

Divorce for Dummies
978-0-7645-7030-8

eBay.co.uk For Dummies, 2nd Edition
978-0-470-51807-6

English Grammar For Dummies
978-0-470-05752-0

Fertility & Infertility For Dummies
978-0-470-05750-6

Genealogy Online For Dummies
978-0-7645-7061-2

Golf For Dummies
978-0-470-01811-8

Green Living For Dummies
978-0-470-06038-4

Hypnotherapy For Dummies
978-0-470-01930-6

Available wherever books are sold. For more information or to order direct go to www.wiley.com or call +44 (0) 1243 843291

12816

FOR DUMMIES®

A world of resources to help you grow

UK editions

SELF-HELP

Cognitive Behavioural Therapy For Dummies
978-0-470-01838-5

Neuro-linguistic Programming For Dummies
978-0-7645-7028-5

Emotional Freedom Technique For Dummies
978-0-470-75876-2

HEALTH

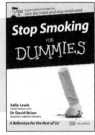

Stop Smoking For Dummies
978-0-470-99456-6

IBS For Dummies
978-0-470-51737-6

Low-Cholesterol Cookbook For Dummies
978-0-470-71401-0

HISTORY

British History For Dummies
978-0-470-03536-8

Twentieth Century History For Dummies
978-0-470-51015-5

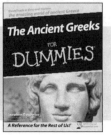

The Ancient Greeks For Dummies
978-0-470-98787-2

Inventing For Dummies
978-0-470-51996-7

Job Hunting and Career Change All-In-One For Dummies
978-0-470-51611-9

Motivation For Dummies
978-0-470-76035-2

Origami Kit For Dummies
978-0-470-75857-1

Patents, Registered Designs, Trade Marks and Copyright For Dummies
978-0-470-51997-4

Personal Development All-In-One For Dummies
978-0-470-51501-3

Psychometric Tests For Dummies
978-0-470-75366-8

Raising Happy Children For Dummies
978-0-470-05978-4

Starting and Running a Business All-in-One For Dummies
978-0-470-51648-5

Sudoku for Dummies
978-0-470-01892-7

The British Citizenship Test For Dummies, 2nd Edition
978-0-470-72339-5

Time Management For Dummies
978-0-470-77765-7

Wills, Probate, & Inheritance Tax For Dummies, 2nd Edition
978-0-470-75629-4

Winning on Betfair For Dummies, 2nd Edition
978-0-470-72336-4

Available wherever books are sold. For more information or to order direct go to www.wiley.com or call +44 (0) 1243 843291

12816_p2

FOR DUMMIES®

The easy way to get more done and have more fun

LANGUAGES

978-0-7645-5194-9

978-0-7645-5193-2

978-0-7645-5196-3

MUSIC

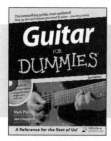

978-0-7645-9904-0

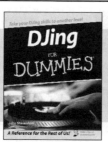

978-0-470-03275-6
UK Edition

978-0-7645-5105-5

SCIENCE & MATHS

978-0-7645-5326-4

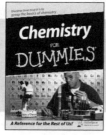

978-0-7645-5430-8

978-0-7645-5325-7

Art For Dummies
978-0-7645-5104-8

Baby & Toddler Sleep Solutions For Dummies
978-0-470-11794-1

Bass Guitar For Dummies
978-0-7645-2487-5

Christianity For Dummies
978-0-7645-4482-8

Filmmaking For Dummies, 2nd Edition
978-0-470-38694-1

Forensics For Dummies
978-0-7645-5580-0

German For Dummies
978-0-7645-5195-6

Hobby Farming For Dummies
978-0-470-28172-7

Jewelry Making & Beading For Dummies
978-0-7645-2571-1

Judaism For Dummies
978-0-7645-5299-1

Knitting for Dummies, 2nd Edition
978-0-470-28747-7

Music Composition For Dummies
978-0-470-22421-2

Physics For Dummies
978-0-7645-5433-9

Sex For Dummies, 3rd Edition
978-0-470-04523-7

Solar Power Your Home For Dummies
978-0-470-17569-9

Tennis For Dummies
978-0-7645-5087-4

The Koran For Dummies
978-0-7645-5581-7

U.S. History For Dummies
978-0-7645-5249-6

Wine For Dummies, 4th Edition
978-0-470-04579-4

Available wherever books are sold. For more information or to order direct go to www.wiley.com or call +44 (0) 1243 843291

12816_p3

FOR DUMMIES®

Helping you expand your horizons and achieve your potential

COMPUTER BASICS

978-0-470-24055-7

978-0-470-13728-4

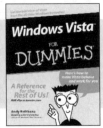

978-0-471-75421-3

DIGITAL LIFESTYLE

978-0-7645-9802-9

978-0-470-17474-6

978-0-470-17469-2

WEB & DESIGN

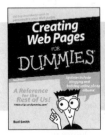

978-0-470-08030-6

978-0-470-11193-2

978-0-470-11490-2

Access 2007 For Dummies
978-0-470-04612-8

Adobe Creative Suite 3 Design Premium
All-in-One Desk Reference For Dummies
978-0-470-11724-8

AutoCAD 2008 For Dummies
978-0-470-11650-0

C++ For Dummies, 5th Edition
978-0-7645-6852-7

Excel 2007 All-in-One Desk Reference For
Dummies
978-0-470-03738-6

Flash CS3 For Dummies
978-0-470-12100-9

Laptops For Dummies, 2nd Edition
978-0-470-05432-1

Mac OS X Leopard For Dummies
978-0-470-05433-8

Macs For Dummies, 9th Edition
978-0-470-04849-8

Networking All-in-One Desk Reference For
Dummies, 3rd Edition
978-0-470-17915-4

Office 2007 All-in-One Desk Reference For
Dummies
978-0-471-78279-7

Search Engine Optimization For Dummies,
2nd Edition
978-0-471-97998-2

Second Life For Dummies
978-0-470-18025-9

The Internet For Dummies, 11th Edition
978-0-470-12174-0

Visual Studio 2008 All-in-One Desk
Reference For Dummies
978-0-470-19108-8

Web Analytics For Dummies
978-0-470-09824-0

Windows XP For Dummies, 2nd Edition
978-0-7645-7326-2

12816_p4

**Available wherever books are sold. For more information or to order direct go to
www.wiley.com or call +44 (0) 1243 843291**

End-User Licence Agreement

You should carefully read these terms and conditions before opening the CD-ROM packet ("Product") included with this book ("Book"). This is a licence agreement between you and John Wiley &Sons Ltd ("Wiley"). By opening the accompanying CD-ROM packet, you acknowledge that you have read and accept the following terms and conditions. If you do not agree and do not want to be bound by such terms and conditions, promptly return the Book and the unopened CD-ROM packet to the place you obtained them for a full refund.

The rights licensed to you under this Agreement by Wiley cannot be transferred or sub-licensed to a third party.

Copyright

The entire contents of the Product are protected by copyright (unless otherwise indicated on the Product). As a user, you have certain rights set forth below; all other rights are reserved.

Terms of Use

You may download, view, save to hard disk or diskette and store or print out the material contained in the Product ("Material") for your own personal and non-commercial use, scholarly, educational or scientific research or study. In addition, you have the right to use brief excerpts from the Material in your own scientific, scholarly and educational works or similar work products (including articles for academic and professional journals) provided you include a notice in the following form:

[figure/table/exercise etc reproduced from [title of Book, copyright year, name of copyright owner/ author] published by John Wiley & Sons Ltd, with permission from the author",

You may not use any of the Material for any commercial gain.

You must seek the consent of the copyright owner in respect of all other use of the Material.

Certain components of the Material may be owned by third parties and you must abide by such parties' terms of use as indicated on the CD-ROM.

Unauthorised and unlawful use of the Material is a breach of copyright.

Except as expressly provided above, you may not copy, distribute, transmit or otherwise reproduce the Material or systematically store such Material in any form or media in a retrieval system; or store the Material in electronic format in electronic reading rooms or print out multiple copies for inclusion in course packs; or transmit any Material, directly or indirectly, for use in any paid service such as document delivery or list serve, or for use by any information brokerage or for systematic distribution of material, whether or not to another user and whether for commercial or non-profit use or for a fee or free of charge.

In order to protect the integrity and attribution of the Material, you agree not to remove or modify any copyright or proprietary notices, author attribution or disclaimer contained in the Material or on any screen display, and not to integrate the Material with other material or otherwise create derivative works in any medium based on or including the Material. This is not meant to prohibit quotations for purposes of comment, criticism or similar scholarly purposes.

Finally, you may not do anything to restrict or inhibit any other user's access to or use of the Product.

Additional Terms

Wiley is not responsible for any charges associated with accessing the Product, including any computer equipment, telephone lines, or access software.

The Product may provide links to third party websites. Where such links exist, Wiley disclaims all responsibility and liability for the content of such third party websites. Users assume the sole responsibility for the accessing of third party websites and the use of any content appearing on such websites.

Warranty Limitations and Liability

(i) THE PRODUCT AND ALL MATERIALS CONTAINED THEREIN ARE PROVIDED ON AN "AS IS" BASIS, WITHOUT WARRANTIES OF ANY KIND, EITHER EXPRESS OR IMPLIED, INCLUDING, BUT NOT LIMITED TO, WARRANTIES OF TITLE, OR IMPLIED WARRANTIES OF MERCHANTABILITY OR FITNESS FOR A PARTICULAR PURPOSE;

(ii) THE USE OF THE PRODUCT AND ALL MATERIALS CONTAINED THEREIN IS AT THE USER'S OWN RISK;

(iii) ACCESS TO THE PRODUCT MAY BE INTERRUPTED AND MAY NOT BE ERROR FREE;

(iv) NEITHER WILEY NOR ANYONE ELSE INVOLVED IN CREATING, PRODUCING OR DELIVERING THE MATERIALS CONTAINED IN THE PRODUCT, SHALL BE LIABLE FOR ANY DIRECT, INDIRECT, INCIDENTAL, SPECIAL, CONSEQUENTIAL OR PUNITIVE DAMAGES ARISING OUT OF THE USER'S USE OF OR INABILITY TO USE THE PRODUCT, AND ALL MATERIALS CONTAINED THEREIN; AND

LICENSEE RECOGNIZES THAT THE PRODUCT IS TO BE USED ONLY AS A REFERENCE AID BY RESEARCH PROFESSIONALS. IT IS NOT INTENDED TO BE A SUBSTITUTE FOR THE EXERCISE OF PROFESSIONAL JUDGMENT BY THE USER.

The Material has been compiled using reasonable care and skill however neither Wiley nor the author of the Product can guarantee the accuracy of such Material and accept no responsibility for any error or misrepresentation. All liability for loss, disappointment, negligence or other damage caused by the reliance on the Material is hereby excluded to the maximum extent permitted by law.

Jurisdiction

This Licence will be governed by English Law as if made and wholly performed in England and the parties agree to submit to the non-exclusive jurisdiction of the English courts.

General

This agreement constitutes the entire understanding of the parties and revokes and supersedes all prior agreements, oral or written, between them and may not be modified or amended except in a writing signed by both parties hereto that specifically relates to this agreement. This agreement shall take precedence over any other documents that may be in conflict herewith. If any one or more provisions contained in this agreement are held by any court or tribunal to be invalid, illegal or otherwise unenforceable, each and every other provision shall remain in full force and effect.

Acceptance Procedure

On installing the Product on you personal computer you will see the following notice which you will need to respond to before being allowed access to the Product.

If you have read and consent to all of the terms and conditions of this Licence, please click the button below marked "ACCEPT". You will then have access to the Product.. If you do not consent, select "DO NOT ACCEPT", in which case you will not be allowed access to the Product.

ACCEPT   DO NOT ACCEPT